The Dictionary of Ornament

THE DICTIONARY OF
ORNAMENT

ALBERT RACINET

STUDIO EDITIONS
LONDON

The *Dictionary of Ornament*
was originally published in 1885
by Firmin-Didot et Cie, Paris
under the title *Deuxième Série de L'Ornement Polychrome*

This edition is published by
Studio Editions Ltd.
Princess House, 50 Eastcastle Street,
London W1N 7AP

ISBN 1 85170 357 8

Printed and bound in Malaysia.

TABLE OF CONTENTS.

EDITORS' PREFACE

Since the main purpose and general plan of this great collection, the second series of which is represented in this volume, has already been expounded in the first series, we shall not repeat them here.

The reader will find a General Introduction at the beginning of the first volume, in which the general principles of ornamental art are set forth, as they have been conceived by the particular genius of each race and transmitted from one civilization to the next.

The structure is identical in both publications, so that the elements which make up the second book hereby enrich and complete the chapters of the first one.

It is in fact to make up for the incompleteness of the first volume, which was so favourably received by a judicious public, that, acceding to the wish of our numerous readers, we have provided a continuation for it, conceived in the same spirit and with the same intention.

Thanks to an additional 120 plates, which bring the total number to 220, we may legitimately affirm that however vast the subject matter may be, nothing that the practitioner should know has been omitted.

Amongst the most remarkable additions which this new collection offers, we would particularly point out several entirely new series, such as that concerning the fascinating field of Slavo-Russian ornamentation, which was brought to light by the Moscow Exhibition in 1883, and which was unknown to us at the time of our first publication. Readers will also note the chapters devoted to various branches of Oriental art and to the many and various artistic products of the Renaissance, the seventeenth, eighteenth and nineteenth centuries.

The reproductions of certain genres, no longer in fragmentary form but complete, such as whole pages of the Koran or of certain pieces of Boulle furniture, are also one of the felicitous innovations of this new series. Furthermore, there are striking examples of the use of the human figure in ornamentation, from the time of the Eygptians and the Greeks, together with the different senses in which it was viewed and the various styles of each epoch and nation.

LIST OF PLATES

IN THE ORDER IN WHICH THEY ARE ARRANGED, WITH THE NAMES OF THE SYMBOLS

BY WHICH THEY ARE DISTINGUISHED.

CLASSIFIED LIST OF THE SUBJECTS CONTAINED IN THE PLATES.

WOVEN FABRICS AND PRINTED MATERIAL.

Materials, Tapestries, Embroideries, Lace, Printed or Painted Cloth or Wall-paper.

CHINESE; pl. VI, VIII and IX. — Japanese; pl. XII, XIII, XIV, XV, XVI and XVII. — Indian; pl. XIX. — Middle Ages; pl. LIII and LVI. — Renaissance; pl. LXXIX, LXXXVII and XCI. — XVth century; pl. XCIV, XCV and CI. — XVIIth century; pl. CIII, CIV, CV and CVII. — XVIIth–XVIIIth centuries; pl. CXII and CXIII. — XVIIIth century; pl. CXIV, CXV and CXVII. — XIXth century; pl. CXIX and CXX.

CERAMICS.

Painted, Glazed, Enamelled Earthenwares; Faiences and Porcelains, Pavements and Wall-facings.

Egyptian; pl. I. — Greek; pl. IV. — Persian; pl. XXVIII, XXIX, XXX, XXXI and XXXII. — Moorish; pl. XXXVII. — Ottoman; pl. XXXVIII. — Middle Ages; pl. XLVI, XLVII, XLVIII and L. — Renaissance; pl. LXXXVIII. — XVIth century; pl. LXXXIX.

MOSAICS.

Greek; pl. IV. — Byzantine; pl. XXXIX. — Middle Ages; pl. XLVI, XLVII and L. — Romano-Byzantine; pl. LIV.

STAINED GLASS.

Middle Ages; pl. LV. — Renaissance; pl. LXXXV, LXXXVI, LXXXVII and LXXXVIII.

IRONWORK.

Middle Ages; pl. XLVIII.

INCRUSTATION, NIELLO AND METAL MARQUETRY.

Indian; pl. XVIII. — Indo-Persian; pl. XXII and XXVI. — Persian; pl. XXVII. — Arabic; pl. XXXIV. — XVIth century; pl. XCVI. — XVIIth century; pl. CVIII, CIX and CX.

GOLDSMITH'S WORK AND JEWELLERY.

Cloisonné Enamel and Other, Enamelled Gold, Jewellery, Chasing.

Japanese; pl. X and XI. — Indian; pl. XVIII. — Indo-Persian; pl. XXV. — Persian; pl. XXVII. — Middle Ages; pl. L. — Russian; pl. LXIII, LXV, LXVI, LXVII, LXVIII, LXIX and LXX. — Middle Ages; pl. LXXII. — Renaissance; pl. LXXIII, LXXIV, LXXX and LXXXIII. — XVIth century; pl. XCIII, XCIV, XCVI and C. — XVIth–XVIIIth century; pl. CII. — XVIIth century; pl. CVIII, CIX and CX.

SCULPTURE.

High and Low Reliefs, Real or Simulated.

Egyptian; pl. I and II. — Greek; pl. IV. — Greco-Roman; pl. V. — Chinese; pl. VII. — Byzantine; pl. XL. — Middle Ages; pl. XLVIII, LIX, LX, LXI and LXII. — Renaissance; pl. LXXXVII, XC and XCI. — XVIIth century; pl. CVI. — XVIIIth century; pl. CXVI and CXVII.

LACQUERED AND PAINTED WOODWORK.

Chinese; pl. VII. — Middle Ages; pl. LIX, LX, LXI and LXII. — XVIIth–XVIIIth century; pl. CXII.

MURAL PAINTING.

Egyptian; pl. I, II, III. — Greco-Roman; pl. V. — Middle Ages; pl. XLVIII and XLIX. — Renaissance; pl. XCI and XCII. — XVIIth century; pl. CIV, CVI and CXI. — XVIIIth century; pl. CXIV.

PAINTING.

Chinese; pl. VIII and IX. — Middle Ages; pl. LXII. — Renaissance; pl. LXXXI. — XVIIIth century; pl. CXVIII.

PAINTING ON MANUSCRIPTS.

Indo-Persian; pl. XIX, XX, XXI, XXII, XXIII, XXIV, XXV and XXVI. — Persian; pl. XXXIII. — Arabic; pl. XXXV and XXXVI. — Celtico-Byzantine; pl. XXXIX, XLI and XLII. — Celtic; pl. XLIII. — Middle Ages; pl. XLIV, XLV, LVI, L, LI, LII, LVII, LVIII and LXII. — Russian; pl. LXIII and LXIV. — Armenian; pl. LXXI. — Middle Ages; pl. LXXII. — Renaissance; pl. LXXIII, LXXIV, LXXV, LXXVI, LXXVII, LXXVIII, LXXX, LXXXI, LXXXII, LXXXIII and LXXXIV. — XVIth–XVIIth century; pl. XCVII, XCVIII, XCIX and X. — XVIIth century; pl. CXI and CXII.

THE HUMAN FIGURE ACCORDING TO ORNAMENTAL STYLE.

Egyptian; pl. I. — Greek; pl. IV. — Japanese; pl. XVII. — Middle Ages; pl. LXII. — Renaissance; pl. LXXXI, LXXXII, LXXXV, LXXXVI, LXXXVII, LXXXVIII, XCI, XCII and C. — XVIIth century; pl. CIII, CIV, CVI, CVII, CVIII, CIX, CXI and CXII. — XVIIIth century; pl. CXIV and CXV.

CARTOUCHES.

Japanese; pl. XVII. — Renaissance; pl. XC, XCI, XCII, XCIII, XCIV, XCIX and C. — XVIIth century; pl. CIV, CV, CVII, CXI, CXII and CXIII. — XVIIIth century; pl. CXV, CXVI, CXVII and CXVIII.

PLATES AND DESCRIPTIONS.

EGYPTIAN.

COLOURED HIGH AND LOW RELIEFS. — PAINTINGS. — MISCELLANEOUS OBJECTS.

By drawing a parallel on this page, between elements so essentially different as colossal statues belonging to great architecture and objects no larger in volume than a perfume bottle, and by placing them next to paintings and bas-reliefs, our purpose is to point out the nature and the abundance of possibilities which the Egyptians had at their disposal, while still retaining the unity of style of their ornament. The serenity expressed in the great statuary was in keeping with the flat design of the creatures and objects represented in the bas-reliefs and paintings. The Egyptians usually confined their interpretation of nature to unnaturalistic forms, but they avoided monotony of treatment by taking a wide variety of species, ranging from man to insect, from plant to bird.

The Egyptian combinations of rectilinear patterns and undulating scrolls are certainly very interesting. Yet, whilst acknowledging their ingenuity in this respect, the fact that the very nature of these combinations is common to many nations should not be overlooked. The repetition of a single motif along the borders, or the filling-up of surfaces with a continuous pattern, is an ornamental expedient known to reed-braiders and weavers everywhere. However, the same is not true of the particularly vital principle which enabled the Egyptians to enrich their ornamentation with representations of fauna and flora. Moreover, the charm of the elements of this genre, found in the monuments of ancient Egypt, is enhanced by the fact that the Egyptian artist drew all his inspiration from local sources. For it is the River-god, the Nile — with its water-lilies, its birds, the scarabs of its silt, its locusts — which engendered this specific world.

An indication of several of the subgroups and of some of the meanings behind the symbolism, should suffice to show the extent of possibilities employed by the Egyptian artist, as well as the general characteristics of his language.

N°s 14 and 15. High-relief. Front and profile view of a pillar-caryatid from the *speos* or temple dedicated to Phre, the sun, at Ibsamboul. In Egyptian architecture, the caryatids are never used as supporting elements, but always lean against the parts of the construction which serve this purpose.

The Ibsamboul temple is one of those troglodyte marvels which were contrived directly in the rock. It is a sandstone mountain, hollowed out and chiseled like a nut-shell: statues, pillars, beams and altars are all carved in the rock. "Picture", said Maxime du Camp, "Notre-Dame de Paris hewn out of one lump of rock."

The figure represented here, the original of which is seven metres tall, is a portrait of Ramses Sesostris. It is part of a set of eight colossi, all identical, which lean against as many pillars, supporting the ceiling of an interior hall or *pronaos*.

Notice the awe-inspiring solemnity of these colossal effigies. This giant with a somewhat oversized head is wearing a *skhent*, made up of a war helmet and a mitre, on which shines the *uroeus*, the royal prerogative. The attributes which he holds are the shepherd's crook, the *pedum*, and the master's whip, the *nekkeh* or *flagellum*, which are the symbols of sovereignty. His only garment is the *schenti*, the tight loin-cloth. Its folds are drawn from the back towards the front and held by a belt, the buckle of which is shaped like a shield, or cartouche, and is joined to a pendant in *cloisonné* enamel ending in a fringe of *uroeus*.

All these statues, as well as the bas-reliefs depicting the feats of the hero which line the walls, are coated with a layer of stucco on which the work of the sculptor was completed, before it was painted over with rich and varied colours.

Every aspect of these figures is typical of the period, from the belt buckle and the eyes of the Pharaoh, elongated by kohl tinting, to the beard which is truly royal. Indeed, the beard of the sovereign, which was in fact a false appendage, trimmed in a square according to the custom of upper-class Egyptians, was longer than that of his subjects. The string which fastens the beard is visible.

The hieroglyphic inscriptions on the pillar behind the colossus exalt the Pharaoh, conqueror of Asia and Africa.

N° 21. Painted bas-relief of great size, representing a seated woman on a throne with a step. Sculptures of this kind are outlined by a contour which is carved in the stone. The paint is laid upon a white coating and the general aspect is that of a fresco. The design is so severely geometric, that the figure's one visible leg completely conceals the other. The head is drawn in strict profile, but the torso is turned so that both shoulders can be seen and the movement of the arms is brought out.

This figure bears the general features common to all the divinities: the *ankh*, symbol of divine life, is held in the left hand, while the right hand carries the sceptre, a simple cane in the case of goddesses, which ends in a lotus' bud, the full shape of which is represented in n° 3.

The *klaft*, or national head covering, is topped by a special head-dress presenting the head of Hathor, the Egyptian Venus, wearing her fillets, such as she is represented on capitals. We have chosen this example to illustrate how the Egyptians overtly transgressed, in certain cases, the usual rules of representation in profile.

Without either cross or sceptre, the distinctive sign of each divinity could be seen on his or her head in the form of a head-dress. With the considerable number of characters who people the Egyptian Pantheon, it was necessary that this indication of the head-dress be of the utmost clarity. This explains why head-dresses which did not lend themselves to a side-view were represented as from the front, even on a head in profile.

Nº 20 alone could account for the usefulness of this type of expedient. It is the upper part of the royal standard of Ramses Sesostris. The figure is a personification of Egypt, bearing on its head two horns, the emblem of generation, between which shines the disc of the sun. Represented in profile this figure would have been incomprehensible.

The human figure is further encountered in paintings nºs 4 and 12, the features of which are non-Egyptian. The purpose of the artist was not only to indicate the origin of the contents of the vessel, but also to explain the nature of the relationships by which these contents were obtained. Nº 4 is a perfume vase characterized by its stopper, and it was probably due to a tribute such as the ones Ramses imposed upon Syria that Egypt came to acquire the perfume it contained. The tormented position of the two kneeling Asiatic figures clearly shows that they are vanquished. Nº 12, on the other hand, indicates that the contents of the vessel which is carried by native Africans, were freely traded.

Nº 6 is another perfume vase, characterized by its heavy stopper. The upper part of the vase is decorated with the heads and necks of two horses which are placed symmetrically. They are adorned like the horses of an Egyptian chariot with rich trappings and ostrich plumes. The vase probably contained one of those reviving ointments used in the grooming of war-horses, either before or after battle.

Nº 13 is a porcelain vase with its own spatula, representing the hedgehog. It probably contained ground antimony. Nº 10 represents the heron; nº 2 the cricket.

Nº 18, a flask which the artist chose to shape like a swan at rest with a curved neck, exhibits both the versatility and the boldness of the Egyptian artist.

Nº 8 is a bas-relief representing the scarab, the sacred dung beetle, which appears on the door of the tomb of Ramses V, at Thebes. The establishment of this insect as the symbol of immortality and fertility may have originated from a natural phenomenon, the great number of scarabs which cover the silt of the Nile after its waters have subsided.

Nºs 1, 3, 9, 16, 19 and 22. Lotus flowers open or in bud, in bouquets or singly, painted or sculptured.

Nº 16, representing a vertical series of lotus flowers which ends in a fine shoot of rose-shaped flowers and spatulate leaves, is one of the most beautiful specimens of lotus paintings.

This design of a flower on its stalk also appears on the fragment nº 5: it is the prow of a boat on which the lotus carries the disc of the sun. The same idea, but with more rigid regularity, was used for the metallic looking-glass, nº 11, a shape in common use. Nº 17 is an enamelled crockery cup agreeably decorated with spear-shaped leaves which embrace the form.

The radiating flowers of nº 7 sag slightly, as they would in a natural bouquet.

Nº 23 is a fragment of a necklace made of lapis-lazuli and gold; it is composed of a series of small spatulas.

These examples are taken for the most part from the great work of Champollion on the monuments of ancient Egypt and Nubia. Nºs 13, 14, 15, 16, 17 and 18 are taken from the portfolio by Prisse d'Avennes.

EGYPTIAN. ÉGYPTIEN. AEGYPTISCH

Lestel, lith Imp. Firmin-Didot & Cie Paris

EGYPTIAN.

SUPPORTING COLUMNS AND PILLARS OF THE PLANT PRINCIPLE.

In Egyptian architecture, because the aspect of the small pillar is that of a simple plant, i.e. with a single stem, and the aspect of the column that of a collection of plants, they belong entirely to the ornamental domain.

The style of the column in the monuments of ancient Egypt is not repeated according to the row in which the column stands, as in our orders or architecture, for each column often has its own distinguishing features and two columns placed side by side may carry different capitals. As Mariette Bey wrote: "Unlike Greek architecture Egyptian architecture is not a mathematical art, in the sense that the different parts of a monument are not precisely proportional to one another."

Egyptian columns, according to the treatises on architecture, are composed of four parts: the block or abacus, the capital, the shaft and the base.

The abacus is always square and its width is that of the architrave it supports. It relieves the capital and prevents it from seeming weighed down by the architrave.

Several shapes were given to the capital. Egyptian architects formed their columns and the ornamentation on them after the model of the lotus, the papyrus and the date-palm. The shaft of some columns grows uniformly smaller from base to capital, while on others it appears slightly swollen with a narrower lower part, like the stem of the lotus after which it was modelled. Moreover, architects imitated the way in which this plant grows by decorating the lower part of the shaft with a herringbone pattern, representing the scales or undeveloped leaves which are found on its stem. The reliefs of carved elements never projected beyond the surface of the column, in order to preserve the purity of its form. The base is always cylindrical and it is usually curved slightly.

The Egyptian floral column is not necessarily divided into separate parts, base, shaft, and capital. Only the abacus which forms the uppermost part of the column is separate. Indeed, the column itself is as unified as the plant or cluster of plants which go to shape it. The closed bud or the flower in bloom which mark the outline of a capital form a whole with the shaft, and the round base coloured like the alluvium of the Nile, is likewise part and parcel of the plant.

More complicated forms of ornamentation belonging to the plant principle succeeded these main types, with a bouquet forming the capital. They are composed of flowers of identical or different species with the buds and open flowers appearing together. These developments seem to have been mainly due to the Greeks at the time of Ptolemaeus, that is at a much later epoch than the age of the objects in our examples.

Nos 1 and 2.

Pillars from the palace of Thothmes III, in Karnak, XVIIIth dynasty. Papyrus and lotus stems with open flowers. Bas-relief.

No 3.

Small pillar used in pavilions of a type dating back to the IVth dynasty, to the age of wood construction. Single stem carrying a bud, at the base of which young shoots are fastened on by a tie bound five times around the shaft, to look like a bouquet.

Nos 4 and 5.

Upper parts of small pillars of the same type but with painted wood.

No 6.

Small pillar from a pavilion. Here the flower is half open, the buds of the young shoots are more mature, making the bouquet appear larger. The tie is characterized by its hanging ends. The abacus, which is usually present with the open flower, does not have the same width as the upper part of the flower but seems to emerge from it. This example, as well as nos 4 and 5, come from various hypogea.

Nos 7 and 8.

Columns of stone buildings. The capitals are shaped like closed buds and carry an abacus as large as the diameter. These shapes are the oldest and most widely used in stone architecture. Here the bud forming the capital is cut off to receive the abacus.

No 7 represents the cluster-shaped column found in the buildings of Amenophis III, in Thebes, and of Thothmes III, in Karnak, who both belong to the XVIIIth dynasty.

No 8, whilst confirming the principle of the cluster, expresses it in a more unnaturalistic manner. This column comes from the Kournah palace, the Menephteum, founded by Menephta I, whose reign followed that of Amenophis III.

In the bouquet of figure no 7, which is fastened by a tie in order to make the group of stems appear like a cluster, the early, small pillars can be seen in their entirety. Each individual stem with its inherent grace is clearly defined.

In no 8, the artist followed the same principle with a greater freedom and enveloped most of the cluster. This modification may certainly be regarded as an important advance, since the detail of stems and buds lessened the scope of possible decoration.

No 9.

Capital found on the columns of the hypostyle hall of the Ramsesteum, in Thebes. XIXth dynasty. We show here both a detail of the top and a general view of the column.

It is with the flower in full bloom forming an opened-out capital that the genre received its ultimate expression, combining grace with strength. We have seen some removal of detail, which was at first partial; here, however, all the stems of the cluster have been eliminated, suggesting the shape of an open flower. In the mind of the artist, this flower presented itself as the silhouette of a bunch of papyrus and lotus flowers on their stems, bending under the weight of the circular disc which they support. This may be seen on the sides of the fine calyx, which bears two rows of painted flowers.

No 10.

Date-palm fronds form this capital, which is also opened out. The joined leaves are moulded into a sort of basket, with the branches providing the decoration. Bunches of dates and even the scales of the trunk sometimes appear on this type of capital, which is found in a wide variety of forms.

The accompanying illustration, which shows the relative proportions of the colossus examined in the preceding chapter and the column, represents a fragment of the Menephteum at Gournah. As the colossus measures seven metres one may infer the enormous proportions of the hall.

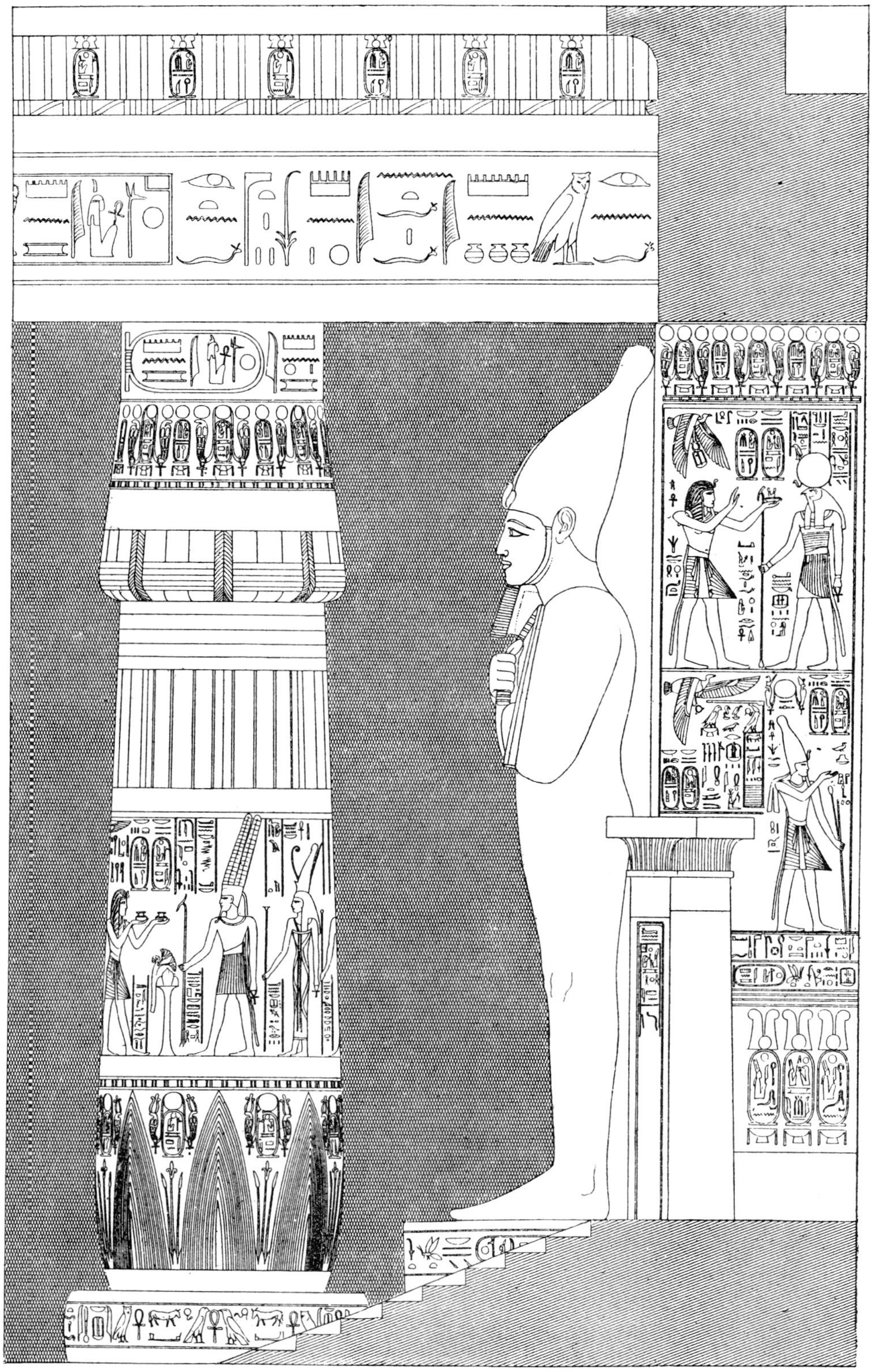

These documents are taken for the most part from the unpublished portfolio left by Prisse d'Avennes, with the rest coming from his great work on Egypt.

Spiégel lith

Imp. Firmin Didot & Cie, Paris

EGYPTIAN.

MURAL PAINTINGS.

CONTINUOUS GROUNDS AND RUNNING FRIEZES. — ORNAMENTATION OF HANGINGS.

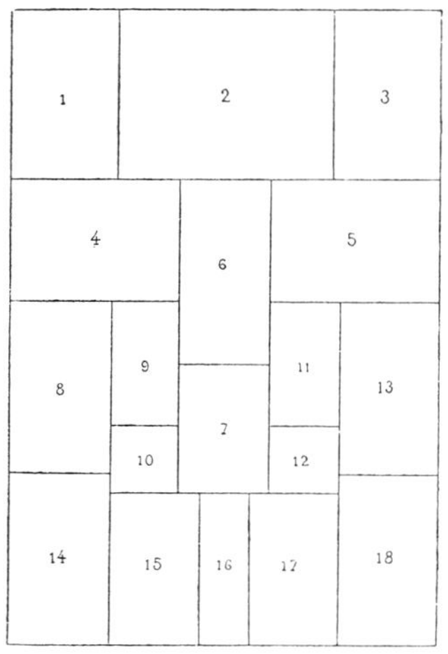

With the exception of nos 4 and 5, all these paintings are ceiling decorations from the necropolis of Thebes and from tombs of various epochs.

Nos 9, 11, and 16

Primitive forms from the XIIth to the XXVth dynasty.

Nos 7, 14, and 18

Guilloches and meanders, from the XVIth to the XXth dynasty.

Nos 8 and 13

Scrolls and fleurons from the XVIIIth to the XIXth dynasty.

Nos 2, 15 and 17

Ox skulls and meanders, XXth dynasty.

Nos 1, 3, 4, 5, 6, 10 and 12

These are without a specified date.

In the plate bearing the symbol of the *goat's head* one may find various sorts of motifs, which mostly belong to the fauna and flora of Egypt. In this plate, however, the motifs belong to the purely abstract realm. One still encounters the lotus flower, yet when this flower is on its stem, the latter loses the aspect of a plant to become ornamental tracery, as may be seen in n° 6. Otherwise, lotus flowers appear only with a cut stem and are used with complete freedom by the artist, who draws solely upon the interplay of lines inherent to the silhouette of the flower, either forming friezes with its repeated image in a single row, as in nos 4 and 5, or placing it in opposite directions on a regular pattern divided by horizontal stripes, as in nos 1 and 3.

With the exception of fragment n° 11, which belongs to the category of reed-weaving, of which hangings were also made, and the friezes in nos 4 and 5, which might have been painted directly on fabric or leather in a manner very common with the Egyptians, all the other examples belong to the technique of appliqué ornament stitched upon a woven or leather ground, forming a composition arranged in a geometrical pattern.

EGYPTIAN.

EGYPTIEN.

AEGYPTISCH

Lestel, lith.

Imp. Firmin-Didot & Cie Paris

GREEK.

THE GREEK STYLE. THE IONIC ORDER. — MONOCHROME AND POLYCHROME.

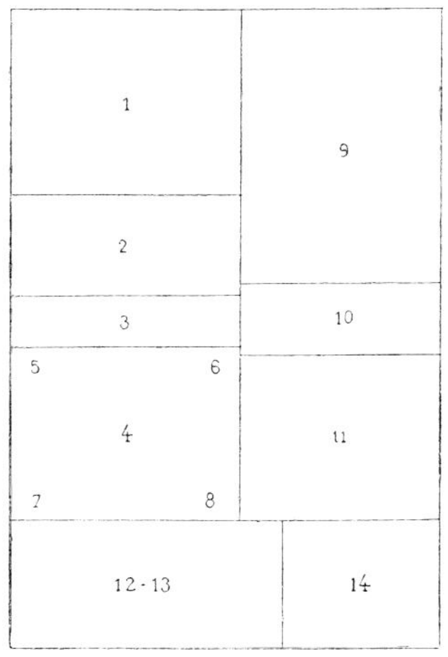

The interest of the delightful fables invented by the Greeks on the origins of drawing and sculpture, which they were by no means the first to practice whatever their claims, is that they offer, as it were, a complete statement of their basic principles on the matter. Saurias of Samos is said to have traced the first silhouette, by outlining on the sand with his sword the shadow of his horse. Koreah of Sicyone, daughter of Dibutades, having sketched on the wall against which he was asleep the silhouette of her lover, supposedly obtained from her father permission to fill up this outline with clay and thus modelled the first bas-relief.

This manner of representing objects and creatures on the basis of their outline, and the attention given to correctly achieving their relative proportions, which was the earliest style of the Greeks, may be considered as the very basis of all their figurative arts as seen in the decoration of surfaces, bas-reliefs, or of paintings on objects.

The draughtsmanship of the Greeks produces an almost magical effect. It submits its subjects, for example the human figure, to a sort of transfiguration by representing it in silhouette and refining its forms. The Egyptians had also sensed the advantages of this process and they used it to draw onto their monuments the images of their gods and heroes, strikingly transfigured into effigies of colossal dimensions. However, it was the Greeks who developed all the possibilities of the genre, since they added to the basic technique their superior ability in portraying the elegance and grace of the human body, to which we owe our awareness of all its beauty.

N[os] 2, 12, 13, and 14, are capitals of the Ionic order (n[os] 12 and 13 being in the same capital seen from the front and from the side). These fragments are from the Wingless Victory and the Erechtheion, on the Acropolis, at Athens, and belong to one of the most interesting periods of Greek architecture.

To colour this type of architecture paints were laid flat along the lines of the design or upon the reliefs, after the manner of the Egyptians. Generally, the surface was prepared with a coating of a mature akin to stucco. Sometimes the tints were formed with encrusted coloured pastes, as can be seen on the Erechtheion; sometimes the colour was provided by mosaics. The ornamented details of these capitals are treated like enamels, the function of which is to set off the double scroll which characterizes the Ionic style.

The variations which exist in the shapes of the scrolls and in the other parts of the top of the column indicate that the Greeks did not necessarily abide by a fixed set of rules when they adorned a column with the features of the Ionic order. Vitruvius relates that the Ionians of Asia had modelled their column after the slender and gracious proportions of a woman, with the scrolls of the capital representing her twisted hair, and the fluting of the shaft the folds of her garments.

Ionic scrolls recalled the custom of suspending the horns of sacrificial animals from the tops of the temples and from the corners of altars. As to the origin of the style, we know that capitals forming a corbel over the column were familiar to the Egyptians, and that the Greeks who had settled on the coast of Asia Minor must have been aware of Assyrian architecture, and especially of the capitals at Persepolis which consist of two half-figures of bulls back to back.

The fragments of pottery decoration shown in n°s 1, 3, 4, 5, 6, 7, 8, 10 and 11, belong to the two main categories of monochrome ornamentation: pottery adorned with yellow figures on a black ground, and pottery adorned with black figures on a yellow ground.

N° 11 is taken from an Etruscan amphora which was found at Chiusi in 1851. It depicts three women warriors retreating from combat. The figures are painted in black on the light tone of the baked clay, and the details have been traced with a sharp point on the black coating. The fullness of movement in the bodies enhances the effect produced by this severe style, and the interplay of draperies and weapons has been discreetly employed here to create a rhythmical link between the figures.

The second genre consists in using the yellowish tint of the pottery for the figures and the ornaments, and covering the rest of the surface with a black colour which creates an artificial background The black lines which delineate the inner details of the figures allow a much greater variety in the poses they adopt which range from pure profile to a certain amount of foreshortening, so as to compose a varied series of silhouettes. According to the laws of human sight, a light colour on a black ground appears to have a greater volume than in the opposite case, and from an artistic point of view it offers richer results. Our fragments, despite their unity of style provide us with examples which display a great variety of expressions.

N° 1 depicts a funeral scene. A small temple, its pediment recalling Selene, the Moon-goddess of Asia Minor, determines the nature of the composition. This temple belongs to the Ionic order, which seems to have been the only order employed for funerary edifices. In paintings on vases the Ionic column always represents a sepulchral monument, and when, as in the present case, there is a dialogue, the seated character is always the deceased, both in bas-reliefs and in paintings. Around the main scene, which is bathed in the light of the moon, figures present offerings, and as the departed is a woman these offerings are a fan, baskets of clothes, a casket and a crown. A mirror, which in these monuments reflects the entire life of the deceased, is held by a man resting his foot on the final mile-stone, and holding the stick which was used for the journey. Among the offerings provided in the tomb, which follow the most ancient custom, are victuals, represented here by the bread-basket and the platter of olives.

The whole scene, which is flanked by palmettes, is regular, the temple occupying the centre. The details, however, are treated with that Greek form of symmetry, *eurythmia*, which consisted not in the repetition of identical things but in the arrangement of equivalent things. The pattern of rosettes, their centres offset in white, has the appearance of a constellation, adding its own discreet and serene light to this funereal scene.

N° 3 is one of those ornaments which formed a decorative ring around a vase. The marine world is here represented by several creatures, including the cuttle-fish, silhouetted in their own element indicated by the small running Vitruvian scrolls.

In fragment n° 4, which depicts Ganymede abducted by Jupiter in the form of an eagle, the artist has employed with great skill the tracery formed by the stems of the plant. These scrolls are very different from the palm shapes and other regular floral patterns of architecture.

N° 10 is the fragment of a Bacchanalia. The movement is particularly remarkable, since the space in which the dance takes place is strictly limited in height. Here, as in the metopes of the Parthenon where Phidias succeeded in fitting human figures in spaces for which they would be too tall if they merely stood upright, the Bacchantes are depicted with great freedom and variety of movement. The Greeks excelled in compositions of this sort, in which the human figure, represented with increasing scientific accuracy and with exquisite taste, is treated as a running ornament. The ornamental foliage on which the Bacchantes conduct their revels is also significant, as in Greece the Bacchanalia was originally an exclusively pastoral celebration.

N°s 1, 3, 4 and 10 are Apulian vases from the Berlin Museum. The Greeks founded several colonies in the southern part of Italy, and the vases from Apulia are related mainly to the cult of Dionysus, the Roman Bacchus, whose worship these Greeks imported into Etruria. The Dionysus of the Greeks, sometimes likened to the Egyptian Osiris, combined in one symbol the wine which gives rise to inebriation and the mystical idea of death and resurrection. In the Roman world he eventually became associated only with the idea of death, as can be seen from the Bacchic representations on many sarcophagi.

N° 9. Bas-relief in mosaic. Decorative plaque. This figure which belongs to the purest Greek style, is a personification of Hope, *Elpis* in Greek, *Spes* for the Romans, which was the object of a specific cult in both nations. Tradition has it that Hope is represented as a young woman, elegantly dressed holding a flower in one hand and slightly raising her garment with the other.

Mosaics of this type were fitted into the wall, where they usually made up a series representing each divinity separately. This bas-relief is believed to come from ancient Metaponte, and one assumes that it formed part of the decoration of some temple or other edifice of the Roman era. Our reproduction being half the size of the original, one may infer the fineness of these types of works as regards the delicacy of the drapery, the outlines of the body, and the flesh tints.

Mathieu lith.

Imp. Firmin Didot & Cie, Paris

GRECO-ROMAN.

MURAL PAINTINGS. — COLOURED BAS-RELIEFS. — *TROMPE-L'OEIL.* — ELEMENTS OF ARCHITECTONIC ORNAMENTATION

THE POMPEIAN PALETTE.

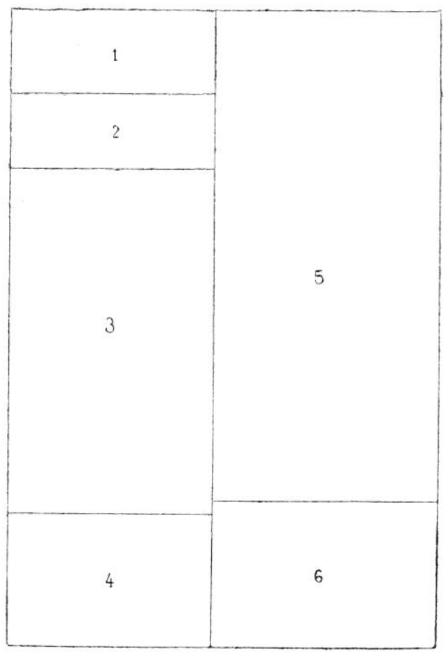

Fragments nos 1 and 2 are from a temple situated close to the forum of Pompeii which appears to have been dedicated to Venus. The colouring is only partial, the stone remaining visible for the most part. The colour acts as a complement to the ornamentation; its function is to emphasize the sections, the outlines, and to set off the small motifs carved in bas-relief.

Nº 3. Architectural decoration painted in *trompe l'oeil.* This example is from a temple which is believed to have been dedicated to Jupiter, and which Mazois includes among the municipal buildings of Pompeii. The buildings of this town appear in some cases to have served a dual function, which in the present case may have been that of a temple and of a storehouse for the public treasury.

Nº 4. Rows of black and brown stones painted on the lower part of a wall, offering a richer combination than the rudimentary base in the previous example. This is a fragment from the walls of the *comitium*, which formed part of the portico of the forum.

Nº 5. This example of an architectonic decoration painted upon a wall is taken from a monument which seems to have been used for feasts in general, such as public sacrifices, or important political events. This is indicated by the victuals which appear on the uppermost part of the painting.

Nº 6. Fragment, the origin of which was not specified by Mazois. It is coloured with the same black as the base of a wall, and it seems to have served as an adornment to one.

Méheux, lith. Imp. Firmin-Didot & Cie Paris

CHINESE.

REAL AND IMITATION EMBROIDERIES. THE INVENTORS OF THE ART OF AN ENTIRE WORLD.

Our two examples were taken from the art of official ceremonial. One is the pectoral of a civil mandarin, the other a fragment from the lower border of a ceremonial robe.

The pectoral is a piece of material attached to the gown, on which are embroidered or painted figures of birds for civil mandarins, and of animals for military mandarins. The animals worn by the mandarins in this way may be real or legendary, and they differ according to rank. The *pu-fu*, or pectoral representing the *fung-huang* (the phoenix of the Chinese), is the insignia worn by civil magistrates of the highest order. The example shown here is the same size as the original.

The scene contained within this little square is both naturalistic and emblematic. It depicts the heaving waves of the sea, a storm with streaks of lightning, and the sun rising from the mist. The *fung-huang* appears against this background as the emblem of resurrection, and probably symbolizes the fertility of the storm.

The fragment taken from the lower part of a ceremonial robe forms part of a circular horizon, the roundness of which suggests that of the earth, which was known to the Chinese. This cataclysm, represented on the gown of the emperor and on that of civil servants, belongs to a general genre. An ingenious emblem, it suggests that out of the chaos of nature there emerge leaders who are in charge of restoring and keeping order.

The scene depicts a flood and a volcanic eruption. The craters of the volcanos are set off by flames, which line the whole background of the scene and are coloured with various substances. Nevertheless, this apparently universal destruction is submitted to the authority of the emperor, whose mighty intervention is indicated by the dragon with five claws, his personal insignia. And with the rose of China trimmed with ribbons, the artist delicately announces that everything shall be restored to its former bloom.

These scenes are drawn in a conventional manner; the fragment of gown is a silk embroidery, the pectoral is a painting, treated in identical fashion since it is an imiation embroidery. The fine silk is already in itself a glossy material, its lustre enhanced by the manner in which it is applied. The paint of the imitation embroidery which overlays it, therefore has equally shiny colours.

Bauer, lith

Imp. Firmin-Didot & Cie Paris.

CHINESE.

ORNAMENTAL MOTIFS PAINTED AND GILDED ON LACQUERED WOODWORK.

As a rule, the characteristics of these ornamentations are similar to those of the bas-reliefs found on Egyptian walls. A carved outline makes the motif stand out from the general plane of the surface. Engraved lines etch out the details, or mark the edges of hollowed out spaces. The Chinese use this process with such skill that they can confer upon the subjects represented in this manner the illusion of a relief: an illusion which they render, as it were, complete, by simulating on the upper parts of the gilding the kind of erosion which time and use would produce by wearing down the projecting elements.

With the exception of this common method, Chinese ornamentation, which is so singularly alive, differs greatly from the rigid decorative style of ancient Egypt. The Chinese express life with a degree of intensity and abundance which is not encountered elsewhere. In both cases, ornamentation is a language, but it is not the same language, and the ingenious, observant Chinese are much more naive than the symbolic Egyptians.

We do know that the two forms of art were contemporary, since Chinese decorated porcelain was found in the ancient hypogea; but there is further evidence continually produced to suggest that the Chinese works date back to even earlier times.

"Every race creates its own language as every bird creates its own song", said Doctor Clavel. Among the hypotheses put forth on the possible origins of the human language, if, during the period of the formation of spoken language, man had to turn to an intermediary language, a visual one, that is, one which speaks distinctly to the eye of a thing or a being not yet named — which could be done only by roughly sketching out the shape of this thing or being — one can surely link to it the origin of representative drawing, examples of which were in fact found on weapons and tools dating back to the remotest past of mankind, the Stone Age.

By examining the variety of this type of ornamentation, motifs inspired by every kingdom of nature, many of which show evidence of immediate contact with the creatures in their element, one finds in their ample and simple expression a direct reflection of what the first attempts at the formation of a visual language must have been: it is not hieroglyphic writing and one does not require a Champollion to understand it.

The variety of subjects to which the Chinese were able to lend a decorative character is emphasized by the sense of motion which they imparted even to inert objects. This we can see by examining the plate. In a setting where the black of the lacquered wood forms an artificial atmosphere, suggesting an ideal blend of air and water suitable for all living creatures, everything floats with a movement which flows from the living world to the inanimate objects which surround it.

Manoury lith. Imp. Firmin Didot & Cie. Paris

CHINA.

EMBROIDERIES, DECORATIVE PAINTINGS.

According to the nature of the objects which they are decorating, the Chinese use two principles of design. Their embroideries, in general, retain the conventional design of ancient monuments, with an equally conventional use of colour, that is to say, with strength, vividness, or harmony. They obtain by this means under broad and synthetic forms, a decorative movement and as it were, an exuberance of expression, which no other ancient or modern nation has been able to produce.

The area of a robe illustrated here (embroidery on a black ground) which represents a sort of monster, is a small sample of their skill in this style; both the design and the colours are conventional.

The second style in Chinese art is that of naturalistic painting. These small paintings (about 50 centimetres in height) consist of only a few elements. In this genre, the entire decoration is composed of the branch of a tree and a bird or a leaf and a flower, which stand on their own in a setting which is always inundated with light.

Sometimes, the composition presents the aspects of a landscape; yet the distant background is merely suggested and the vividness of the decoration is never affected by it.

The vertical panels displayed here belong to a kind of painting that was very popular. They simulate the narrow aperture of a window, through which the viewer can see only a fragment of the outer world, glimpsed as if by chance. The Chinese and the Japanese, who were so often inspired by the same genius, excelled at these bright and cheerful compositions, in which the silhouettes of things and creatures are usually outlined on the same plane against a peaceful, luminous background.

Small paintings of this sort, painted in water colours, were used to decorate houses, in which they were hung in sets of two, three or six, called *kwa-pin* or *tyvo* or even twelve, called *wei-pin*.

CHINESE CHINOIS CHINESISCH

Picard lith. Imp. Firmin-Didot & Cie Paris

CHINA.

NATURALISTIC PAINTINGS, EMBROIDERIES, PRINTED FABRIC.

As in the plate identified by the symbol of a *lute* this page contains various expressions of Chinese ornamentation, which was followed more or less closely by the Japanese, according to the genre in question, namely, painting on silk or on paper, embroidery, or printing on fabric.

In addition to the vertical naturalistic painting, there is here a larger scene depicting the branch of a tree in blossom on which a bird is perched. This example is typical of the bright, airy, even poetical style at which the Chinese and Japanese have proven to be so inventive. The two panels with a black ground are embroideries which form a completely different kind of natural ornament. The plants, flowers, birds and insects are all set off against this black ground by colours of varying degrees of brightness, to which the lustre of the silk conveys the greatest brilliancy.

The panel with a brownish crimson ground belongs to a loftier order. The design, which is compartmentalized, is printed with the ground itself, and the decoration is given variety and life by the addition of several flat tints. In this style, the particular harmony of the decoration is subordinated to the ground, following the rules of good chromatics. One may recognize here the experienced eye of those who produced the most beautiful enamels in the world. The legendary bird in the centre of the motif is the *fu-huang*, which belongs to classical ornamentation.

Chataignon, lith.

Imp. Firmin-Didot & Cie. Paris

JAPAN.

DECORATIONS IN VARIOUS METALS. HILTS, RINGS AND HANDLES OF KNIVES AND SABRES.

"There exist", says M. Aimé Humbert, "no jewellers or goldsmiths, properly speaking, in Japan. The products which are closest to the workmanship of the gold and silver smith, are the decorations on the weapons of the Yakounines. All sorts of adornments are used to enrich, in an essentially peaceful style, the handle, the hilt and the sheath-rings of both their two sabres, as well as the metal handle of the knife which accompanies these arms" (*Le Japon, voyage de 1863–1864*).

To decorate these narrow surfaces, the Japanese used gold, silver, steel, copper, and a composition known as *sawa metal* which can be divided into *shibushi* and *shakudo*. The various metals are inlaid, and their treatment is completed by carving and chasing.

The objects reproduced in the accompanying plate speak for themselves and require no further emphasis from us on their technical merits. Some of these examples are true marvels of skill and taste.

We have deemed it unnecessary to retain the narrow central hole in the hilts, through which the blade is set. This opening is never given any specific adornment, and nothing links it to the whole decoration.

P. Lestel, lith.

Imp. Firmin-Didot & Cie. Paris

JAPANESE.

THE METALLIC PLAQUE.

ORNAMENTATION ON ARMS AND OBJECTS OF DAILY USE.

This plate is a continuation of the previous plate bearing the symbol of a *level*, with the addition here of pommels and several examples taken from miscellaneous objects.

The Japanese, who do not wear personal jewellery, like to decorate many household utensils and even furniture, with fine metalwork of this kind. They apply it to medicine-boxes, silver teapots, chests of drawers, smoking-pipes, flower-vases, diversifying it with all the hues of gold, silver, or copper, combined and modified in a hundred different ways.

No chemist has manipulated metals with such skill as the Japanese gold and silver smith. None, by the effect of acids and salts, has modified the surface of bronze or silver in the same way as the craftsman from Kioto, or Kanga, who buried in the ground, or plunged into the sea the copper vase or the silver cup inlaid with niello, which would not be taken out of its hiding-place until oxidation was complete, even if the process took ten or twenty years.

Among the means employed by the Japanese to confer so great a richness upon their metals, instead of purifying their crude copper as our chemists do, they deliberately leave in it traces of sulphur, arsenic, iron or lead, and may even add to it substances of this nature. From measured mixtures of lead, for example, they obtain purple copper, black copper, green copper, which we do not have; and these alloys are named *shido*, *udo* and *seido*. They are intrinsic colours, which in this genre must be distinguished from the colourings of the surface of the metal, which required yet another operation.

Lastly, the richness of colour in Japanese ornamentation is in harmony with the richness of the design, as may be noticed on our plate.

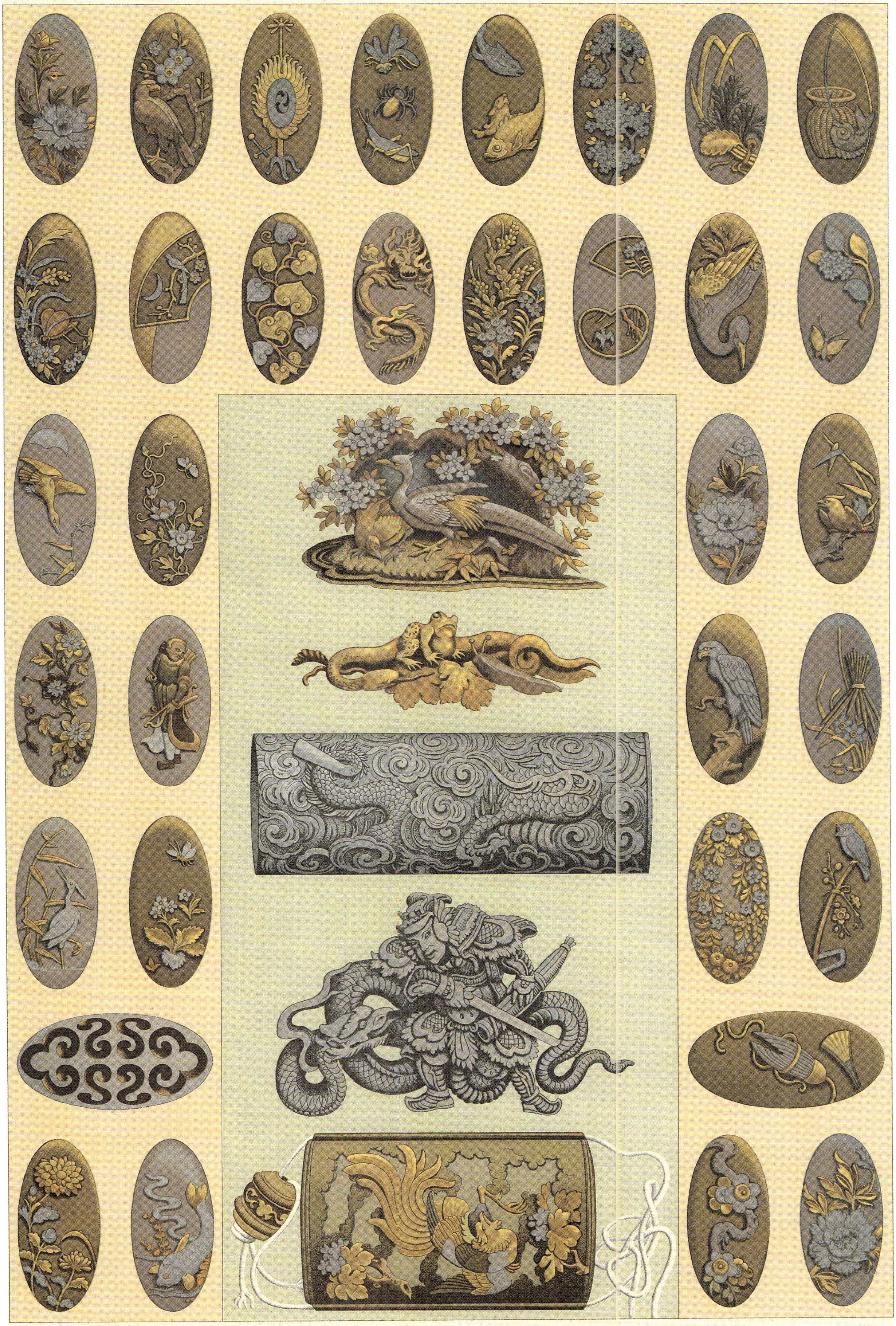

Lestel, lith. Imp. Firmin Didot & Cie Paris

JAPAN.

DECORATION OF FABRICS. — THE FOLDING-SCREEN WITH ONE HUNDRED SAMPLES.

Among the various techniques used by the Japanese to decorate their screens, one of them consisted in arranging on them samples of various brocaded and woven fabrics. These fragments are set out in a quite regular order, the motifs remaining independent from one another.

The motifs gathered here were taken from two of these folding-screens bearing one hundred samples. No written information about Japanese manufacturing techniques could be as reliable as these, since the fragments were taken from products in use in the seventeenth and eighteenth centuries.

JAPANESE. JAPONAIS. JAPONESISCH.

Lestel, lith.   Imp. Firmin-Didot & Cie. Paris

JAPANESE.

DECORATION OF ANCIENT FABRICS.

These motifs belong to the series of examples which make up the plate bearing the symbol of a *pair of bellows*, and they are taken from the same source: the multi-patterned folding-screen. With unfailing good taste they follow the same principle of soft tints and discreet harmonies. Certain motifs recall the primitive weaving and handiwork of the Pacific Islanders, made with fibres of plants and braided reeds, or adorning the wood of paddles and of certain utensils.

JAPAN. JAPON JAPAN

Lestel, lith. Imp. Firmin-Didot & Cie Paris

JAPAN.

WALL-PAPER. CURRENT MANUFACTURE IN CHINA AND JAPAN.

Printed wall-paper for the decoration of dwellings was used in China and Japan much earlier than here, and differs from our painted papers both in its decorative style, and in its old-fashioned method of manufacture. Rather than being made in the form of a continuous sheet which is then divided into rolls for sale, it is block-printed in small sizes and on hand-made paper. Escayrac de Lauture gives the dimensions currently used over most of China as 0.346 metres by 0.266 metres, and 0.994 metres by 0.625 metres. The five examples on the lower part of our plate, come from originals varying in size from 0.45 metres by 0.30 metres to 0.47 metres by 0.35 metres.

Given this method, the patterns are seldom wide or full, since the relative smallness of such strips of paper means that the size of ornament frequently encountered on our wall-paper would be too large. Moreover, in combining patterns the Chinese and the Japanese are quite inferior to the Persians, whose decorative juxtapositions are so ingenious.

Nevertheless, it is with a remarkable balance, a truly superior wisdom, that the Japanese decorate their wall-paper. They renew the wall-paper in their houses at least once a year, a custom which demands that the product remains at a low price. It may therefore be supposed that this need for economy is not unrelated to the sober nature of the colours in the fine prints decorating the modest dwellings of China and Japan.

With the exception of the fragment depicting the small blue birds, the examples on the lower part of our plate are made up of only two tints. The mat grounds are laid down with a brush, the metallic tints by some similar means.

In addition to these economical sheets of paper, which are widely used, printed paper is also manufactured, which by its sheer quality, as well as by the superimposition of numerous colours, is truly a product of luxury. The example on the upper part of our plate belongs to this category. The paper, which is very firm, is of superior quality; the ground is laid down with a brush, perhaps in several coats for the layer is thick and seems almost burnished. The original of this sheet measures 0.62 metres by 0.50 metres; the workmanship is much less rudimentary and economical than in those illustrated below. This depiction of vines entwined round the slender branches of a tree uses a number of blended colours, in the veins of the leaves, the roundness of the fruit, and the contours of the florets, all of which are marked in silver.

The Chinese and the Japanese sometimes use a continuous design, with perpetual repeats, which requires only one engraving, as in the three models in the middle of our plate; they also sometimes print the plates three by three, or two by two, as in the models on the lower part of our plate.

Schmidt lith. Imp. Firmin Didot & Cie. Paris

JAPAN.

VIBRANT DECORATION ON A FLAT SURFACE.

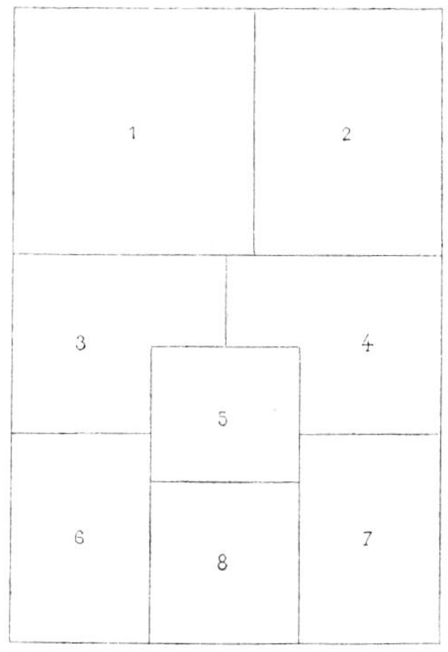

The Japanese excelled in producing by simple means a variety of effects on flat surfaces, such as fabric or wall-paper. Our plate gathers together several specimens of a genre which may be referred to as their vibrant decoration.

N° 1 consists of a symmetrical pattern of identical decorative points on a uniform ground. This is one of the most rudimentary and primitive types of ornamentation, yet it is remarkably rejuvenated by the present motif.

N° 2, a dark black design on a light black ground, consists of the opposition of curving lines forming what one may call undulations.

N° 3 offers another application of the principle of undulations, superimposed on an independent ground with the addition of ramifications.

N° 8 offers a combination of diamond-shaped forms.

N° 4, with its fast-flying birds, outlined in white against a vivid blue sky, seems to suggest that the bodies of the birds are almost ethereal.

N° 6 seems to have been inspired by the twinkling of the stars.

N° 7 appears to resemble those ephemeral suns revolving round an axis with light shooting from them, which one sees in fireworks.

Lestel, lith. Imp. Firmin-Didot & Cie Paris.

JAPAN.

ORNAMENTATION ACCORDING TO THE POPULAR ARTS.

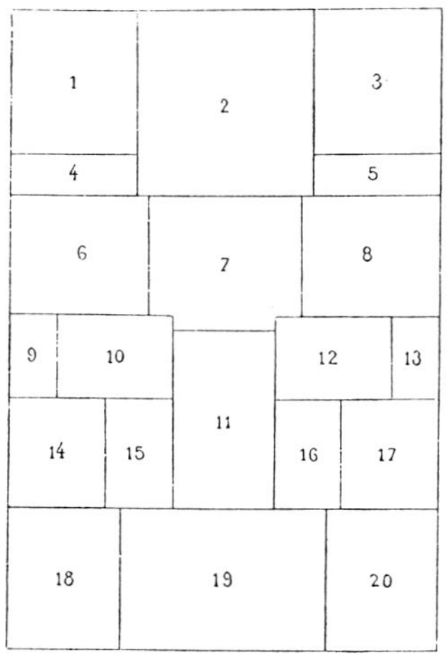

Among the motifs assembled here, some are merely abstract speculations, such as meanders, interlaces, striations, and so on. We do not know whether these patterns bear a symbolic meaning, or whether by combining these symmetrical, continuous designs, the Japanese artisans intend to refer to Him whom Plato names the "eternal geometer".

Moreover, it would be inappropriate for us to seek out the subtle meaning of Japanese symbols, our knowledge being very incomplete on the matter. Nevertheless, we may at least indicate that the pretty fragment nº 19, with its fluttering butterflies, appears to come from a ceremonial bridal gown. The symbolic nature of this piece is explained in M. Aimé Hubert's account of his journey to Japan. "During the wedding ceremony, the young bride moves forward escorted by two bridesmaids, whose role is to flutter from one group to the other, and to do the honours of the table. They are called the male and female butterflies. It is required that in the cut and in the embroideries of their gowns, made of crêpe and gauze, they wear the image of that charming couple which nature, according to popular belief, has used as the symbol of conjugal felicity."

The crane is one of the most frequently encountered images in Japanese ornament. It is a symbol which appears to have manifold meanings, and is always used in the wedding ceremony. In our albums we encounter a crane in the shape of a disc, in the style shown in example nº 2, but merely gilded, on the *norimon* of a bride, and the partitions of the bridal chamber are adorned with images of cranes in pairs.

Our second example shows a combination of three fine cranes enclosed within a hexagon and composing an ingenious decoration suitable in nature to a mosaic.

Lestel, lith.

Imp. Firmin-Didot & Cie, Paris

JAPAN.

CARTOUCHES.

The Japanese often employ cartouches in the Chinese manner, by scattering them on a scene which is thus put into the background. Otherwise, they place cartouches on the corners of their maps. Rarely does the cartouche figure alone. The features of these ornamentations differ greatly from those of our own cartouches.

As may be noted here, it is by a simple contour that the Japanese delineate the form of their cartouches, which are often peculiar in shape.

This style, so widely used by the Japanese, is especially suited to representing a decoration whimsically thrown upon a surface. One of our examples has the shape of the *carta* — the open scroll displaying a subject between its rolled-up ends — which is similar to the use we make of cartouches. However, the Japanese artist, with his taste for the fantastical, gives strange shapes to some of them: a butterfly with its antennae, a sitting bird or a crouching rabbit, and even a skull with holes for the eyes and nose. The more reasonable shapes are those taken from the plant world, the leaves of water plants, and sword hilts. The most common figure is that of the folding fan or the stiff fan. Sometimes the shapes are geometric, simple and regular.

The inner decoration of these cartouches is generally unrelated to their shape. As if they were some sort of aperture, they most often depict landscapes — including the one in the shape of a skull. Sometimes, the cartouche is a mere frame of inscriptions, which remains flat or which appears to be rolled only because it is shaded in various colours. At other times, a cartouche in the shape of a fan will exhibit only the hint of a decoration, such as banks of clouds.

Most often, the human figures which appear are portrayed with a grimace. The Japanese, who are so skilful at capturing the ridiculous aspects of the human species, as is evident from their ivory figurines, seem to set so little value on the beauty of human forms that the ornamentalist never represents them. They perceive beauty in animals and draw it with remarkable accuracy and delicacy, particularly when it comes to winged creatures. But as regards human beings, they are interested in their antics, and the grimace of the fool is what seems to have the most charm for them.

Charpentier, lith. Imp. Firmin Didot & Cie. Paris

INDIAN.

ENAMELLED COPPER OBJECTS, *CLOISONNÉ* ENAMEL, ENGRAVING IN NIELLO AND CHASING ON STEEL.

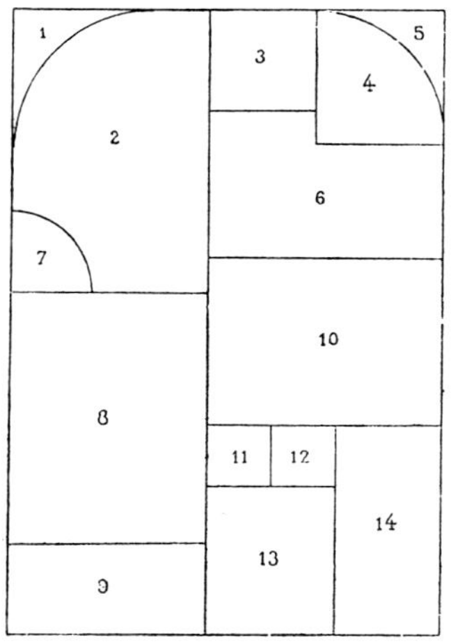

As a rule, ornament on copper objects varies according to the parts to be decorated, such as the outer curve of a vessel, or the inner surfaces of dishes and cups. The divisions on circular surfaces are generally placed at regular intervals between the centre of the object and the circumference. In the two types of combinations, represented by n°s 2, 4, 8, 10, 13 and 14, the ornamentation forms a continuous pattern, with the repetition of a basic motif.

N° 14 is silvered copper.

The pattern in n° 4, in which a sort of flame adorns a series of petals of two alternating types, belongs to a style which may have resulted from an encounter between Arabic and Tibetan artists.

N°s 7 and 9 are taken from Indian armour. The steel is chased and the designs gilded. In n° 7, the gilding is outlined by black engraving.

N° 3 is a jewel made of enamelled gold. As already mentioned, these examples are reproduced in their original size, and this particular piece shows the delicacy of the cloisonné, which is seldom employed with so great flexibility in the treatment of a human figure. Works of this type are very highly valued, the enamels of Rajputana being not only the finest in India, but perhaps the finest in the world.

N°s 1, 2, 3, 4, 5, 6, 8, 10, 13 and 14, are from objects which belong to the Trocadero Museum.

Schmidt, lith.

Imp. Firmin-Didot & Cie, Paris

INDO-PERSIAN.

APPLIQUÉ DECORATION. PAINTED MOTIFS.

The main fragment in our plate is from a decoration of Indian workmanship, the original of which is in South Kensington, composed of appliqué set on fabric and trimmed by white piping cord. In this fine patchwork, the white piping outlines all the pieces of appliqué, large and small. It marks their inner divisions and provides stems for the flowers, which appear more or less vibrant according to the intensity of the background. This piping cord functions in the same way as cloisonné and its passage throughout the decoration serves as a link between all the colours, by conveying an overall tone to the whole. The design is strictly symmetrical and, following Indian taste, covers the entire cloth.

The borders shown alongside this Indian fragment are of the Indo-Persian style, as is the motif on the lower part of the plate, the original of which is painted on the fabric of a tent. These five examples are taken from the fine sixteenth-century manuscript folios in the Trocadero museum. The motifs in the plates distinguished by the symbols of the *horse's hoof* and the *cheval-glass* come from the same source.

INDO-PERSIAN. # INDO-PERSAN. INDO-PERSISCH

Schmidt lith. Imp. Firmin Didot & Cie, Paris

INDO-PERSIAN.

DECORATIVE PATTERNS.

These fragments are taken from several very large paintings which depict historical and legendary scenes forming a series, the key to which is still unknown. They are thought to date from the sixteenth century. These paintings, some parts of which are seriously damaged, are at the Trocadero museum.

Taillefer, lith.

Imp. Firmin-Didot & Cie Paris

INDO-PERSIAN.

DECORATIVE PATTERNS.

These motifs form a continuation to the preceding plate. They are taken from sixteenth-century paintings in the Trocadero museum.

INDO-PERSAN

INDO-PERSIAN

INDO-PERSISCH

Lestel lith.

Imp. Firmin Didot & Cie Paris

INDO-PERSIAN.

PAINTED ORNAMENTS. — RUNNING BORDERS.

The motifs in this plate are taken from the same source as the Indo-Persian ornaments in the plates bearing the symbols of the *horse's hoof* and the *cheval-glass*. Borders, of which this plate is composed, are of great importance in this style, which uses border patterns so frequently in the friezes and lintels of architecture as well as in tapestries.

A certain number of the backgrounds here are of indigo. In India, this colour usually suffices in paintings and tapestries to produce the effect of black, in the place of which it is often used.

Taillefer. lith. Imp. Firmin-Didot & Cie. Paris

INDO-PERSIAN.

ORNAMENTATION OF MANUSCRIPTS. — DECORATION WITH DOUBLE TRACERY.

This page from a fifteenth or sixteenth-century edition of the Koran, in which the splendours of Oriental decoration are so brilliantly exhibited, owes its general features to a pattern of double tracery. This type of pattern, which is only rarely encountered in ornamentation of this style, consists in a basic construction of the flowered scroll motif typical of the Persians and Indians, with a superimposition of more abstract tracery.

Schmidt, lith.

Imp. Firmin Didot & Cie, Paris

INDO-PERSIAN.

ORNAMENTATION OF MANUSCRIPTS.

This plate was taken, as was the preceding one, from a fifteenth or sixteenth-century Koran. The ornamentation is characterized by its wide margin, in which interlocked black and gilded grounds create a pattern of alternating florets, clearing delineated by being outlined in white.

INDO-PERSIAN

INDO-PERSAN

INDO-PERSISCH

Lemoine lith.

Imp. Firmin Didot & Cie, Paris

INDO-PERSIAN.

ORNAMENTATION OF MANUSCRIPTS. CLOISSONNÉ ENAMEL.

This outstanding example of page decoration is taken from an edition of the Koran. It was painted by Mir-Imad, the leading calligrapher of Shah Abbas I in the early seventeenth century, who also produced the fine marginal arabesques in the plate which bears the symbol of the *corset*.

The fine Persian dagger, of which we represent the handle, the top of the pommel, a fragment of the damascened blade, and the sheath, is one of those weapons which are true works of art. It is made of ivory, inlaid with metallic wires which form the scrolls and the divisions of the enamelled ornamentation.

The other dagger which belongs to an older period, is decorated in raised enamel of Indian workmanship. It is a product of Rajputana, home, as we have already mentioned, of the finest enamels in India. It measures 44 centimetres in height and is part of a collection in Saint Petersburg.

INDO-PERSAN

Schmidt, lith.

Imp. Firmin-Didot & Cie Paris

INDO-PERSIAN.

MINIATURES. COPPER ENAMELLED IN NIELLO.

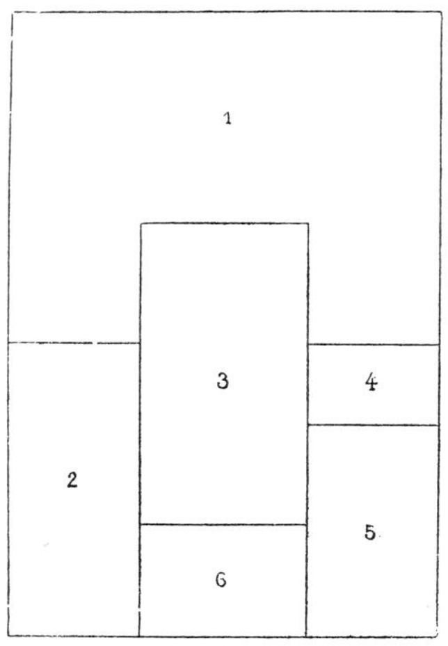

All these miniatures are reproduced in their original sizes. The remarkable disposition of the main motif in example nº 1, which depicts one half of an ornamental frame (the other half being omitted for reasons of space), represents a window frame with a rolled silk blind originally used as a setting for a miniature half-length portrait of an Indian nobleman. This style of ornamental framing for miniature portraits is quite typical.

Nos 2, 3, 4 and 5 are paintings on manuscripts, each displaying a main motif bounded by borders. These ornamentations have the same characteristics as fabric decorations. The borders look like braids, while the large traceries resemble white piping, appliquéd on embroidered grounds.

The running pattern shown in nº 6 is a form of engraved and painted decoration found on a horn.

INDIAN·PERSIAN

INDO-PERSAN

INDISCH·PERSISCH

Bauer, lith.

Imp. Firmin Didot & C[ie] Paris

PERSIAN.

TINWORK DECORATED WITH GILDING AND GEMS. GILDED AND SILVERED ENGRAVED AND PAINTED WORKS OF COPPER.

We shall examine in this plate works made of tin. N° 14, shown here in its original size, is an example of tinwork damascened and adorned with gems. This magnificent product of a system of coloration based on tin is likely to confound what may be regarded as our prejudices concerning the use of cheap metals.

In France these prejudices are such that, with regard to the celebrated tin work of François Briot, many reasons have been put forward to account for the fact that his masterpieces were made of so vile a metal.

The first hypothesis was that Briot had chosen tin in order to preserve his works from any possibility of that future destruction to which most objects made of precious metals are destined. Another suggestion was that these works were models made for the gold and silver smiths of the time. However, these explanations were not entirely satisfactory. Benvenuto Cellini, in his *Treatise on the Goldsmith's Work*, advised all practitioners of the art who wished to keep a specimen of their silverwork, to make copies in lead or tin. At certain eras, moreover, the use of these economical metals was common when the artist wished to display his composition at a preparatory stage, to the patron who had commissioned the finished work.

The tin objects, which François Briot sometimes signed with his medallion bearing the inscription *sculptebat Franciscus Briot*, were cast in great numbers, and the sculptor put the finishing touches to them. They are neither personal samples nor preparatory economical models, but works of art fashioned in a range of tones for which the artist had a particular preference, a predilection shared by other artists as well. Boulle in his finest inlaid works preferred tin to the brightness of silver, while Briot may have chosen tin as being more fusible and malleable than silver.

Among the engraved copper works in the plate, the reader may note a pair of birds in a medallion, set face to face in the ancient manner of the Persians and Syrians. N° 13 shows a repeat of a pattern with medallions in the shape of a quatrefoil, which we have left blank, since the fine etchings in the original were entirely independent from the ornamental pattern. All sorts of scenes might be placed in them, notwithstanding the proscriptions of the Koran, as well as heraldic animals.

N° 1 is from a brass cup damascened with silver (Bibliothèque Nationale, in Paris.)

All the other fragments are taken from tin objects in the museum of Saint Petersburg.

Schmidt. lith.

Imp. Firmin Didot & Cie Paris

PERSIAN.

ENAMELLED AND GLAZED FACING TILES.

In general, brick forms the basis of construction in central Asia. It is adorned with stucco, marble, and more particularly with enamelled and glazed tiles.

These ceramics in the shape of rectangular tiles were juxtaposed so as to form a brilliant patchwork, which was all the richer because each tile was not uniformly coloured as in the mosaics, but contained in itself one element of an endless arabesque, confined only by the lines or the forms of the architecture.

The interest of the examples assembled here and in the plate distinguished by the symbol of the *flower-pot*, resides in the fullness and clarity of their design. They present, on a much larger scale, elements identical with those of the rich illuminations described above as Indo-Persian. This close relationship may easily be explained, since it is the Parsees who, in India, wield the paint-brushes of the miniaturist. Hence, the art of Mahometan India is that of Persia itself.

The most complete expression of this form of ornamentation is found on monuments of the sixteenth and seventeenth centuries, dating from the times of the Sufi dynasty. Shah Abbas, aided by the peace which he was able to confer upon his people, was one of the greatest of all builders. The munificence of this sovereign left so profound an impression on the country, that when a traveller inquires about the name of the founder of some ancient monument, the answer is invariably and often erroneously: "It is Shah Abbas the Great".

This style of ornamentation owes its character to the proscriptions of the Koran, which forbid the representation of living creatures. It dates back to the epoch when Persia, delivered from the yoke of the Arabs, towards the eleventh century, recovered its freedom of expression.

Our documents are taken from the portfolio left by Prisse d'Avennes. Most of them are without any specified origin.

N° 1.

This fragment is 54 centimetres in height. It forms part of the coping of the mihrab of an abandoned mosque in Damascus.

N° 2.

Fragment of a panel, 24 centimetres in height.

N° 3.

Running border, formed by a series of tiles measuring 25 centimetres.

N° 4.

Running border, composed of a series of tiles measuring 14 centimetres. The join is at the base of each flower.

N° 5.

Tile which forms the basis of a continuous pattern. The original is at the museum of Sèvres. Height, 32 centimetres.

N° 6.

This fine fragment is composed of a coping border, of a framing border, and of a continuous pattern confined within the frame. The tiles of the coping decoration measure 22 centimetres lengthwise; the tiles of the framing border measure 25 centimetres lengthwise, the join being in the middle of the rosette, and there is one tile designed for the corner; while the square tiles forming the continuous design measure 25 centimetres on each side.

Schmidt, lith. Imp. Firmin-Didot & Cie Paris

PERSIAN.

ENAMELLED GLAZED TILES.

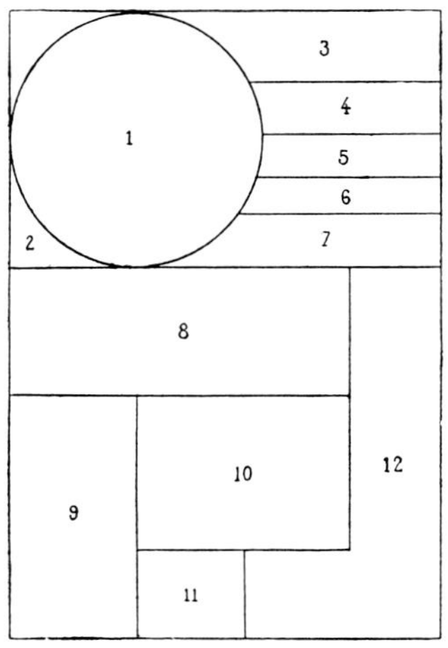

Of all the colours, blue is by far the most frequently employed for the decoration of Persian tiles, particularly those designed for the adornment of interior walls. There are several reasons for this.

All the colours prepared for enamelling are bonded to the metal by firing. Following firing, green, yellow, crimson and carmine tints may emerge very different, whereas blue never loses its beauty.

These documents are taken from the portfolio left by Prisse d'Avennes.

Original sizes.

Nº 1.

Dish with a flat centre. Glazed earthenware. Diameter, 32 centimetres.

Nº 2.

Corner motif.

Nº 3.

Running border, each tile is 16 centimetres in length.

Nº 4.

Running border, each tile is 24 centimetres in length. The join falls in the middle of each rosette.

Nº 5.

Running border, each tile is 15 centimetres in length. From the mihrab of an abandoned mosque in Damascus, which was converted into a gun-powder factory.

Nº 9.

Each tile is 29 centimetres in height and the join is placed between the ends of the shields. From the mihrab of the same mosque.

Nº 10.

From the same mosque. The fragment shown is 32 centimetres in height.

Nº 6.

Running border, tile 17 centimetres lengthwise.

Nº 7.

Running border, length of fragment shown, 50 centimetres.

Nº 8.

Running border, length of fragment shown, 50 centimetres.

Nº 11.

Border with a cable pattern, height 6 centimetres.

Nº 12.

Border of a frame, with one corner tile. This fragment measures 52 centimetres.

PERSIAN. # PERSAN. PERSISCH

Schmidt, lith. Imp. Firmin Didot & Cie, Paris

PERSIAN.

MURAL DECORATIONS.

GLAZED TILES FOR FACING INTERIOR AND EXTERIOR ARCHITECTURE; THE METALLIC PALETTE.

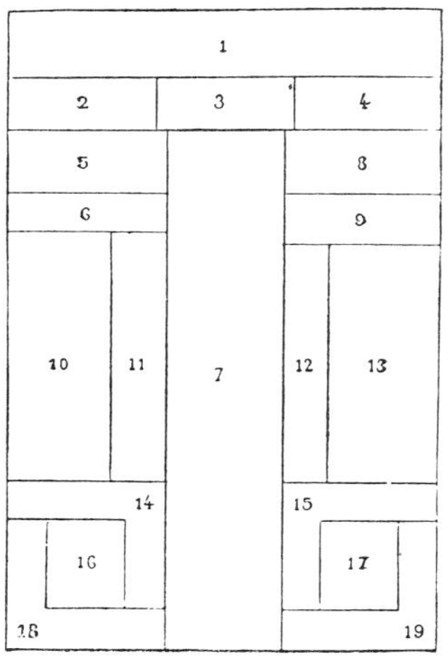

Nos 1, 13, 16 and 17 are fragments taken from the palace of the Sultans at Konieh, the former *Iconium*, capital of the Seljuks. This town, which was wealthy, for it is located on the caravan route which runs from Mesopotamia to Smyrna, has been reduced to the rank of a provincial capital.

The magnificent palace which provided us with these motifs now lies in ruins, and the examples reproduced here are from the final remains of the large reception hall, or *selamlik* of the Sultans.

Nos 16 and 17. Flower-shaped decorations from the interior of the pendentives of the cornice, which is made of stucco. As the flower shapes which fill up the flat surface inside each pendentive are of various shapes, it is believed that no moulding was used in their making.

All the other motifs, which are of a different style, come from the decoration of a mosque at Tabriz, in the province of Anatolia. Notwithstanding the proscriptions of the Koran, which forbade the use of gold for the adornment of religious edifices, in the Tabriz mosque the walls and the pillars were adorned with gilded ornaments.

The glazed tilework used in the facings of walls is in general made of a porous, lightly baked clay. The clay seems to have been fired twice: once to bake it, a second time to fix the ornamentation. The metals used for the colours are generally cobalt for blue, manganese for purple, lead-protoxide for yellow, sulphured lead for white, and oxidized iron for the red, which is always yellowish. Green is usually obtained with lead, although some appears more emerald green, possibly because it is made from a sort of copper. The tile is first given a ground in a plain colour, and on this the running ornamentations are applied by means of a mould. The colour is always fairly thick.

These documents are taken from the works of Charles Texier's *Déscription de l'Asie Mineure* and *Voyage en Perse*.

Bauer, lith

Imp. Firmin-Didot & Cie, Paris

PERSIAN.

ENAMELLED OR GLAZED TILEWORK.

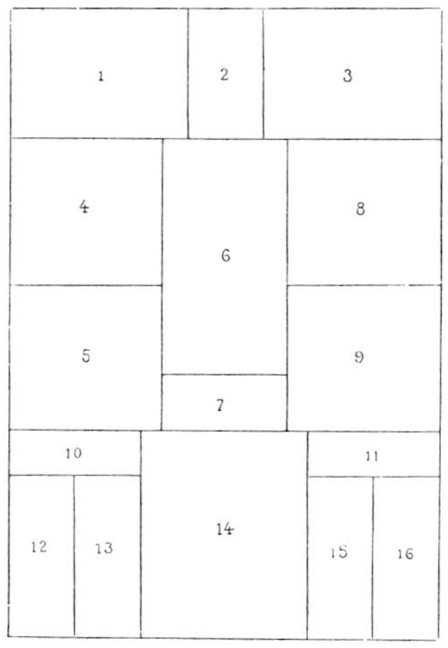

It was in conformity with ancient traditions that the inhabitants of Asia employed brilliant facings for the adornment of their interior and exterior architecture. In the wooden palace of the mythical Pheacian king, described in *The Odyssey* as having been decorated with polished metal sheets, and "shining as brightly as the moon or even the sun", it is possible to recognize the Median style, which was practiced by the Chaldeans, the Phoenicians, and the Assyrians.

Alongside this custom of metallic ornament on wooden buildings there existed another tradition, that of brick construction faced either with thin slabs of stone on which variously coloured bas-reliefs were sculptured, or with large enamelled bricks forming mural paintings. We have given examples of these enamelled bricks in the Assyrian plate of our first series, nos 6, 7, 8, 9 and 10.

The disadvantage of these constructions made of bricks that were simply sun-dried was their lack of durability. Indeed, Babylon and Nineveh are now nothing but desolate mounds of bricks spread out on a few arid hills and plains devoid of vegetation.

Nevertheless, the technique persisted and Islamic monuments present, in their turn, a spectacle similar to that of Assyrian constructions. The concern of the Persian architect was different from that of the Egyptian architect, who preferred to employ limestone and granite, so as to confer upon the monument a greater durability than that of mere sun-baked clay. In Asia, a coloured and glittering architecture was sought after above all else, and was achieved through the display of splendid arrangements of tiles, which produced those golden palaces, and blue, green, and pink mosques. This type of arrangement is especially rich, since it is composed not of the insignificant mosaic tile, but on the ingenious basis of a form of ornamentation which through juxtapositions, becomes an endlessly ramified pattern contained only by the forms of the architecture.

The illustration below shows the astonishing effects which an artist is able to achieve by combining one kind of tile, into a large decoration.

N° 14, which measures 10 centimetres square in the original, can only be seen to full effect when used to form a pattern of sixteen by sixteen juxtaposed tiles, forming a whole which measures 1.60 metres square.

Amongst our documents, n° 6 is made up of shaded colours, unlike the usual practice of laying pure tints flat on the surface.

These sorts of facing are made in all dimensions, and even for objects. The latter type is represented by fragment n° 2, which is here reduced to one-third of its original size.

N°s 1 and 3 are found in the museum of Sèvres. All the others were exhibited by the Union centrale des arts décoratifs and formed part of the Exposition orientale of 1869.

The second illustration, which follows, displays a pure plant-like pattern, designed in the conventional style.

It is based on tile n° 5, but fitted together in a different way. In this case there are two basic tiles, on which a single design is disposed in two symmetrical directions, one the mirror image of the other. Tile n° 9 belongs to the same system and the tiles are fitted together in the same manner.

PERSIAN PERSAN PERSISCH

Bauer, lith.

Imp. Firmin-Didot & Cie Paris

PERSIAN.

ENAMELLED OR GLAZED EARTHENWARE.

Persian artists excelled in varying the decoration on their earthenware whilst employing only a small number of basic elements, the interplay of single arabesques or conventional flora coloured with flat tones.

N° 1.

Diameter of the original, 40 centimetres.

N° 2.

Diameter of the original, 38 centimetres.

N° 3.

Diameter of the original, 28 centimetres.

N° 4.

Diameter of the original, 27 centimetres.

N° 5.

Diameter of the original, 30 centimetres.

N° 6.

Diameter of the original, 37 centimetres.

N° 9.

Diameter of the original, 40 centimetres.

N° 10.

Diameter of the original, 37 centimetres.

N° 11.

Diameter of the original, 12 centimetres.

All these earthenware products were exhibited at the Exposition orientale, organized at the Champs-Elysées by the Union centrale, in 1869.

The two tiles shown as n°s 7 and 8, the first of a type which can be fitted into a continuous pattern, the other from a running ornamentation along a frieze, are of the sixteenth century. They come from the mosque of Omar, Qoubbet-es-Sakhra. N° 8 is one of the finest types of enamelled and glazed tiles employed in facings.

Durin, lith.

Imp. Firmin Didot & Cie, Paris

PERSIAN.

PAINTING ON MANUSCRIPTS.

MARGINAL DECORATIONS ACCORDING TO THE NATURE OF THE TEXT.

These marginal decorations are taken from a magnificent manuscript of the poetry of Saadi, who was born in the late twelfth century, and is one of the greatest poets of Persia. The calligraphy was executed by Schams at Schiraz, and the paintings which date from 1609, the epoch of Shah Abbas I, are by Mir-Imad.

The delicacy of the marginal decorations represented here is in no way comparable to the loose brush-strokes of those mediocre illuminators who have too often been used to replace them. Each of our borders are constructions, in which long, slender scrolls are evenly distributed on a bright ground. Two of these margins are composed of entwined plants, whose swirling shapes are developed on a single plane. The other two present two distinct interlaced patterns which are superimposed, the plant-like one beneath. The predominating tone is of that fine lapis-lazuli blue most generally found in Persia.

As can be seen, the religious proscriptions which forbade Muslims from representing living creatures, including plants, did not prevent the ornamentalist from achieving outstanding results. Victor Hugo would certainly not have disapproved of so pretty a decoration for the margins of his *Orientales*.

Spiégel, lith. Imp. Firmin-Didot & Cie. Paris

ARABIC.

DAMASCENING. CAMEO ORNAMENTATION.

The Oriental etcher first engraved in intaglio the design to be inlaid, then made little notches with a pin on the edges and bottom of the hollow, to secure the strip of gold or silver wire he would use for the damascening.

Although the technique of Oriental damascening is very ancient the oldest known vases of engraved and damascened copper, brass, or alloyed metals, date back no further than the twelfth century. The twelfth and thirteenth centuries have indeed produced many engraved objects, fashioned both for Muslim princes and for the Frankish barons of the Syrian colonies. This art reached its peak of perfection in the thirteenth century. Two distinct schools of damascening may be distinguished: that of Mossul or Djezareh, and that of the Syrian school, whose main workshops were located in Damascus and Cairo.

It was in Mesopotamia, where the Muslim spirit lost much of its fanaticism at an early period, that the school of Mossul was formed. The most striking characteristic of this style is its use of human or animal figures, whereas in Damascus and Cairo artists were confined to pure ornamentation and to arabic characters. It was only towards the middle of the thirteenth century that objects from these workshops were adorned with heraldic animals, such as the eagle. The vases made for the Franks were sometimes decorated not only with human figures, but even with religious subjects and Christian symbolism.

These decorations were applied on a wide variety of objects, such as large bowls, cups, chandeliers, lamps, dishes and other utensils.

Schmidt, lith.

Imp. Firmin-Didot & Cie, Paris

ARABIC.

PAINTINGS ON SACRED MANUSCRIPTS.

These ornamentations are taken from a single copy of the Koran, the *Glorious Book*, according to the expression of Mohamed. This one is a magnificent copy in all respects. Its size is exceptional, each page measuring one metre in height and fifty centimetres in width. In the original all these cartouches represented here measure no less than thirty centimetres in length. The paper is made of that fine cotton pulp tinted a sort of salmon-pink and polished to a brilliant shine, which the Orientals used at an early period.

This manuscript, which dates from the fifteenth century, or possibly even from the fourteenth century, is truly Arabic only in the nature of the text, for it is Persian in its detail.

Each one of the principal divisions of this Koran (its one hundred and fourteen *surahs*) is preceded by an inscription of the kind shown here.

Oriental inscriptions are often written in Cufic characters, the primitive alphabet of the Arabs, which differs from free-flowing handwriting and owes its name to Cufa, a city of ancient Chaldea where it may have been invented. Cufic has a hieratic shape and it recalls the hand of the prophet, as Mohamed used this alphabet to set down his revelations.

Among the various types of character in the inscriptions shown here, that known as rectangular Cufic may easily be distinguished. The shapes of its symbols are often in themselves ornamental motifs. The characters of this alphabet are indeed so exceedingly ornamental, that Christian architects of the Middle Ages and the Renaissance sometimes went so far as to employ them in religious monuments, for example on the halo above Christ's head.

Ornamentation need no longer be symbolic when the written word is the subject of decoration. Furthermore, if an ornamental hierarchy exists, it would seem natural that the most sumptuous decorations be especially devoted to inscriptions quoting the Word of God.

The luxury of the cartouches in this Koran is thus particularly appropriate, for the illumination of manuscripts differs according to the nature of the texts. The ornamentation of the margins of a Koran, which contains isolated rosettes and Arabic points, belongs in principle to the stellar type. The text affirms that which the represented astral world merely suggests. The symmetrical ornamentation of the inscriptions reflects the order of the universe, its luxury that of the richness of the Creation. Furthermore, alongside those words which codify precepts of all sorts, are the soothing phrases designed to remind the faithful of the supreme felicity of Paradise. The latter are often written in rhyming prose of such perfection, according to the Muslims, that it could not have been achieved by man. The beauty of the ornamentation therefore also reflected this perfection.

ARABIAN. ARABE. ARABISCH

Lestel, lith.

Imp. Firmin-Didot & Cie Paris

ARABIC.

PAINTING ON MANUSCRIPTS. ORNAMENTATION OF INSCRIPTIONS.

This page is a continuation of the motifs in the plate bearing the symbol of the *thermometer*, which provides several types of complete ornamental cartouches. The fragments reproduced here are treated on a larger scale, so as to facilitate a study of the detail. They exemplify the various aspects of the ornamentation of Cufic characters, which are mostly employed in these inscriptions, sometimes isolated, sometimes superimposed upon foliated scrolls.

Notwithstanding its conformity to the proscriptions of the Koran – which had transformed the ancient Zoroastrian who previously treated all sorts of figures into, as it were, an artist with clipped wings – and the introduction of the Arabic alphabet instead of the Chaldean one, the "Arabic" manuscript which provided these specimens is above all a Persian work.

We have included in our first series under the rubic *Arabic* two plates of fragments taken from this same manuscript, which is why we have included it here. However, since the nature of Oriental works has now been exposed to increasingly enlightened criticism, it is necessary to indicate clearly what we mean by the term Arabic art.

The justification for attributing to the Arabs the architectural forms and the style of ornamentation found in Muslim countries has been strongly contested by Adalbert de Beaumont, who points out the relationship between the Byzantine and the Persian styles, and states: "One must therefore unhesitatingly attribute to the Persian nation, which was so refined, so eminently artistic, the glory of the renaissance which led immediately to the Byzantine, then to the Arabic, then to the Gothic styles. The Byzantine cupola, the arch, the vault and that whole pyramidal architecture had been employed by the Persians for centuries."

"By establishing themselves in Asia", says M. Beaumont, "the Romans discovered a brilliant civilization with existing arts, and an architecture which had been formed of old, in which gold, mosaics, enamelled tilework, ivory and gems added the vividness of colour to the beauty of shape." According to M. Beaumont the degenerate taste of the Romans was completely renewed in Byzantium. As for the Arabs, when their time came and once they had settled, they summoned those Byzantine architects, who were the inheritors of both Greek and Persian architecture.

At the time of their greatest strength, the Arabs took advantage of a movement which they had by no means initiated. These nomads have no architectural tradition of their own, and their ban on the representation of all living creatures could only be a hindrance to the arts. The notion of Arabic art is thus increasingly problematic. Prisse d'Avennes published a splendid collection under the title of *Arabic Art*, yet amongst his two hundred plates, most of those which represent miniature ornamentations are purely Persian productions.

Bénard, lith. Imp. Firmin-Didot & Cie, Paris

MOORISH.

COLOURED AND GLAZED MOSAICS. ENAMELLED BRICKS.

The architecture known as Arabic presents in the monuments of Algeria, from where our specimens are taken, an expression which differs substantially from the ancient architecture of the eighth and ninth centuries, as exemplified by the famous mosque of Cordoba and by the mosque of Ibn Touloun in Cairo. Girault de Prangey noted in those parts of the mosque of Cordoba which post-dated its erection an important transformation. He ascribes this change to some political upheaval, and believes the introduction of adorned stucco and of glazed tiles, which replaced the brilliant mosaics of Byzantium, to have resulted from another civilization than that which had erected this monument.

Amongst our examples, n° 5 is especially remarkable for its distribution of colour over two-dimensional designs. This creates the illusion of two superimposed planes, the large octogons set at regular intervals thereby appearing to be secured under an overlying network.

These examples, which were exhibited in 1876 at the Palais des Champs-Elysées, are from the district of Oran and were taken from seven different sites:

1. The surrounding wall of Mansourah (1299 to 1307).
2. The mosque of Mansourah, near Tlemcen (1335–1337).
3. The ruins of the mosque of Sidi-Ben-Issak, in the former cemetery of Semuse, located between Tlemcen and Bou-Medina (fourteenth century).
4. The minaret of Sidi-Bou-Medina, near Tlemcen (1339).
5. The minaret of Agadir, at Tlemcen (1283).
6. The former palace of the M'dersa Tashfinya, at Tlemcen (1335–1340).
7. The gate of the M'dersa of Sidi-Bou-Medina, near Tlemcen.

Amongst these monuments, the minaret of Sidi-Bou-Medina has retained its fine mosaics, which almost entirely cover the upper part of the minaret, thus producing a splendid effect. N° 1 comes from this site.

The monumental entrance door of the former palace of the M'dersa Tashfinya is decorated with magnificent mosaics of enamelled glazed tilework and with very rich pavements. Our n°s 3 and 4 belong to these ruins, several halls of which are now used as warehouses. The entrance of the M'dersa of Sidi-Bou-Medina is likewise adorned with very fine mosaics made of enamelled glazed tilework, which are quite well preserved; our n°s 5, 6 and 8 are from this monument and from the above-mentioned.

Lastly, fragments n°s 2 and 7 offer interesting examples of the characteristic designs formed by simple enamelled bricks being placed on end and in a regular arrangement. They are from the ruins of the mosque of Sidi-Ben-Issak.

Lestel, lith. Imp. Firmin-Didot & Cie. Paris

OTTOMAN.

ENAMELLED GLAZED MURAL TILES; PAINTED ENAMELLED EARTHENWARE.

MARQUETRY.

The facing tiles represented in the accompanying plate are made of common clay covered with a coating of kaolin. This clay is similar to that which the potters of Kutanieh still use today to make their enamelled tiles and their small enamelled pots. Sometimes, as in Yeshil-Djami, the tiles were modelled in relief or hollowed out, before being covered or filled up, as the case may be, with variously coloured enamels. The design thus formed was outlined with a copper substance which emerged black after firing, and which prevented the various enamels from intermingling, as in the technique of *cloisonné*. Sometimes, on the other hand, they were enamelled in slabs, which were then divided into pieces in order to form mosaics.

This fine workmanship declined following the wars which ruined the town of Isnik, where most of the manufactories were located. The technique of painted enamelled tiles has nevertheless been preserved at Kutanieh; yet sadly only the technique remains, for the artists have disappeared.

It would be superfluous to dwell further on this type of ornamentation, which is an offshoot of Persian art. It later degenerated under the influence of French artists who imported the Pompadour style into the Ottoman empire, attracted by the reputation of the magnificence of Sultan Ahmed III.

The splendid central decoration, constructed around the Arabic point, is the sole ornament of a panel, the rectangular ground of which we have had to reduce in size. The four small motifs placed on either side of it are not glazed tiles, but marquetry work from the ruins of monuments in Cairo. Those which represent the same ornament alternately in black or in a light colour, are most highly valued.

Schmidt. lith.

Imp. Firmin-Didot & Cie. Paris

GRECO-BYZANTINE.

PAINTED ORNAMENTATION AND MOSAICS; IX-XIIth CENTURIES.

Nos 2, 3 and 4.

Motifs taken from a Greek manuscript painted in Asia Minor around 800 A.D. (*Gospels, Acts and Epistles*, Greek manuscript, no 4, Bibliothèque de l'Arsenal, in Paris).

This manuscript offers an example of Greek ornamentation modified by Middle Eastern influence. The motifs we have taken from it, which may be regarded as the first expressions of a new art, are the true origins of all the schools of painting on vellum, comprising the Lombard, German, Visigothic and Saxon schools.

These ornamentations, silhouetted on the surface of the vellum or on golden grounds, retain something of ancient Greek clarity, and their broad, rational floral shapes often differ from those on antique vases solely in the nature of the flowers or fruits depicted.

In short, as regards both small productions and large-scale decorations, ornamental technique remained almost the same in both the western and the eastern Greek schools. In principle a restrained liberty and a discretion in coloration governed the work of both the illuminator and the mosaic-maker. The artist simply varied single tones on golden grounds, while on the mosaics, so widely used by the Byzantines, the number of colours in the ornamentation is strictly limited.

No 1.

Mosaic of colossal dimensions serving as a ceiling to one of the aisles of Saint Mark's, in Venice (ninth century).

The above discussion of the general characteristics of the ornaments of the Greek school applies equally to this fragment, which belongs to a Byzantine style more sober than the Oriental, and as discreet as the art of Antiquity.

Nos 5 and 6.

Ornamental border of a page in the shape of a portico, found in a manuscript of the library of Grenoble which was painted in the tenth century, probably in Lombardy. It is considerably inspired by the Greek style. This manuscript is attributed to the Lombardo-Greek school, from 650 to 1100.

Nos 7 and 8.

Ornamental borders of a page with an interplay of ribbons retaining in their angular forms the features of Greek meanders. They are taken from a German missal of the early twelfth century (Bibliothèque Nationale, no 55, in Paris).

No 9.

Motif in the style of the twelfth-century Norman school.

GREEK-BYZANTINE

GRECO-BYZANTIN

GRIECHISCH-BYZANTINISCH

Debénais lith.

Imp. Firmin Didot & Cie Paris

BYZANTINE.

THE NEO-GREEK STYLE FROM THE IVth TO THE VIth CENTURY. COLOURING BY BUILDING MATERIALS.

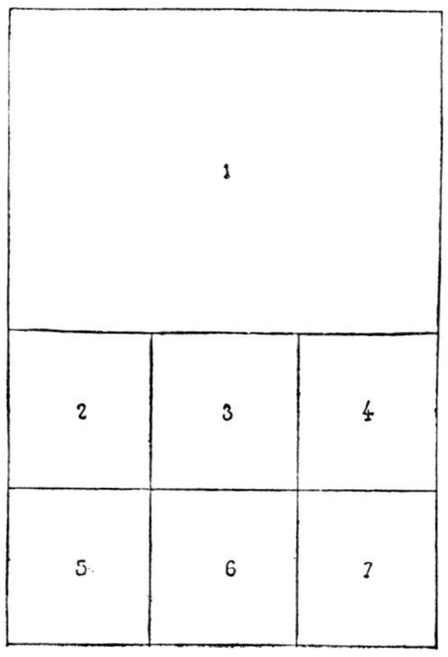

Nº 1.

Fragment of the door of a Coptic church in old Cairo, attributed to Saint Helena, mother of Constantine.

This church, which is used by the Copts, is dedicated to Saint Sergius. According to Maxime Ducamp (*Le Nil, Egypte et Nubie*), it is an indifferent church, adorned with mediocre Greek paintings and with a few wooden sculptures. The crypt below it is well preserved and obviously very old; tradition has it that the Holy Family took refuge there during the flight to Egypt.

This door is made of Egyptian sycamore wood which is also known as "Pharaoh's fig-tree". It was considered by the ancient Egyptians to be poisonous and free from decay, and they employed it for mummy-cases.

Nºs 2, 4, and 6.

Openwork in marble found in San Vitale, the cathedral of Ravenna. Nºs 2 and 6 are decorated openings in the wall; nº 4 is part of a pavement. They all follow the principle of the continuous pattern and are contained by frames with full borders.

Nºs 5 and 7.

Rectangular windows decorated with openwork forming a complete design. These motifs are found in Sant Apollinare Nuovo; each one is encompassed within a full marble border.

Nº 3.

Circular window or bull's eye characteristic of the façades of churches, from the basilica of Pomposa. These openings existed of old in Latin basilicas. The bull's eye is the origin of the Gothic rose-window.

This window is made of variously coloured materials. The oldest examples of this type are to be found in Greece and in the Arabic countries. In ancient Neo-Greek edifices, frequent use is made of alternating stone and brick, white and black, or white and red.

The Cathedral of Ravenna, which was built at the same time as Santa Sophia in Constantinople, is a case in point. It is certain that San Vitale was built by Greek architects, and that Santa Sophia was built by Anthemius of Tralles and Isidor of Milet.

The Greek builders of the late Roman Empire who worked in Italy conferred upon their monuments a particular style which is found nowhere in Latin buildings and which belongs indisputably to the Byzantine school.

The foliage and interlacing of this period are not very salient, and they offer the special features found on most western monuments of the twelfth century.

Photographic documents. Nº 1 is taken from the portfolio of Prisse d'Avennes.

Schmidt, lith.

Imp. Firmin Didot & Cie. Paris

CELTICO-BYZANTINE.

TYPES OF DECORATIVE PAINTING, VIth–IXth CENTURIES.

ENAMELLED METALWORK, Xth CENTURY.

COLOURING OF ROMANESQUE ARCHITECTURE, XIth CENTURY.

FROM ILLUMINATED MANUSCRIPTS.

The title under which we present these ornaments is justified by the scrolls and leaves of the exfoliated Byzantine style, the human figure in the Greek style, and the Celtic interlacing either in the form of simple lacing or terminating in animal heads, which may be seen in n°s 1, 2 and 4. These examples are from Sweden, Denmark, England and Rhenish Germany.

These are not simply evidence of Greek and Byzantine styles rejuvenated by Celtic additions. It is clear that the representations of the human figure are strongly related to the traditions of Greek art, the decadence of which can easily be explained in such troubled times. It is no less clear, as some acute archeologists have pointed out, that in paintings such as n°s 2, 3 and 4, there exists a very direct link between the expression of physical beauty, as the Greeks conceived it in their idealization of serenity, and the expression of moral beauty as the Christians conceived it.

However, the human figure who appears in the centre of these decorations is not the man of the Greeks, but a radically new man who brings the good news of the Gospel and is ennobled by sanctification. It is his image which is set upon the walls of the old Latin basilica. Like the Roman magistrate, who dispensed his justice in the apse of the basilica, before it was adopted as the model of the Christian temple, the evangelist in n° 2 sits in the curule chair. The justice of which he speaks, however, is not part of human law, but heralds eternal redemption.

N° 2 represents the type of chapel found at the extremity of each aisle of a basilica. Its depth is emphasized by curtains, which are twisted round pillars, in the manner of those represented in the mosaics of San Vitale in Ravenna. The vault is adorned with a shimmering pattern of running scrolls above the angel of Saint Matthew who holds the sacred book. The evangelist is seated in the curule chair, displaying a partly unrolled parchment, on which one may read the beginning of his narrative: "*liber generationis*", "the book of the generation of Jesus Christ".

Although this page from a missal contains all the elements of a large-scale mosaic, it seems more likely that it was modelled on the type of painting which replaced more costly mosaics in the many wooden basilicas being so swiftly erected and constantly rebuilt after fires had destroyed them.

Despite this relationship with mosaics of the Constantinian style, the rustic temple, judging by this scene, may have offered the expression of a generally more human Christian ideal than the luxurious temples in which, as in San Vitale, behind the drawn curtains of the mural paintings, the imperial effigies of Justinian with his wife and near relations appear in their grandest array.

In the emblematic scene, nº 4, there is almost no symbolic language. It depicts the archangels Saint Michael and Saint Gabriel, holding the staff of the Greek messenger and presenting an inscribed board which heralds the Gospel of Saint Matthew.

Nº 1. Type of enamelled metalwork, ninth or tenth century. This initial adorns the first page of a psalter written in Latin, which belongs to the British Museum (nº 2904). The book of David was one of the most venerated sections of the Bible and its psalms were adorned, in each monastery, with particular sumptuousness.

According to the traditions of the early Middle Ages, the artist drew his inspiration from the most luxurious objects of his time, the enamelled gold pieces which must have been most familiar to him.

Golden objects in the shape of a letter seem to have been common in those times. Among others, an old tradition relates that Charlemagne presented twenty-four abbeys with reliquaries in the shape of a letter of the alphabet.

Our capital B may therefore have existed in reality, although it matters little whether this product of the goldsmith's skill was actually nailed upon a wooden structure or not, for it offers a complete model, an indication of the techniques of that time, which succeeding centuries merely continued, including Benvenuto Cellini, despite his claims.

Enamelling, as the Byzantines practised it, is the simple application onto metal surfaces of vitreous materials, which are bonded by the process of fusion. The colours of enamel have an extraordinary vividness, and never decay. It seems that the Byzantines learned the art of enamelling from the Orientals, and that they began practising it around the time of Justinian, in the sixth century, in a way which then seemed entirely new. Indeed, the technique of *cloisonné* enamel, which was primarily used by the Byzantine goldsmiths, is quite unlike the thin coating of vitreous material which the Greeks, and more particularly the Etruscans, applied with a blow-pipe on certain extremely delicate jewels.

Enamel lends itself to the representation of all sorts of subjects. Over the course of several centuries, sacred or profane figures representing Christ and his mother, the principal saints of the Oriental Church, the emperors and their wives, and so on, were reproduced *ad infinitum*. At the time of Leon the Isaurian, in the early eighth century, the worship of images was prohibited and as a result the human figure could not be reproduced on any of the objects used in schismatic temples. Furthermore, the severe persecution enforced by the iconoclasts led to large-scale emigration of Byzantine artists, who brought first to Italy and then to the rest of Europe their native arts and their unique skills.

Thus, in an encounter between those who came from Byzantium and those who, as the Celts, had come from Asia long before the expatriation of the Greek goldsmiths, the Celtico-Byzantine style had its origins. The English refer to it as the Anglo-Saxon style, and it is generally given the name "Carolingian", because of the period when it attained its perfection.

The example here precisely illustrates that kind of enamelled metalwork being practised around the tenth century in the monasteries of England; for in the early Middle Ages, this technique was essentially pursued by monks. All the wealthy abbeys possessed a goldsmith's workshop, and some of these became true schools to which monks from other monasteries came to learn their craft from renowned masters.

Before enumerating the various techniques displayed in this example, let us first recall that enamel is glass coloured by metallic oxides which sometimes leave it translucent, sometimes render it opaque, and which requires an adequate preparation of the metal on which it is laid, according to the purposes for which it is being used.

The techniques brought together here are as follows:

1. The technique of *champlevé*, also called *taille d'épargne*, in which each hollow is filled with enamel and fired: this is the old Egyptian technique.
2. *Cloisonné* enamelling, in which the various colours are separated by metal wires soldered to the metal surface.
3. The technique of *basse-taille*, in which the design is first engraved in the metal, before being covered with transparent enamel which grows darker according to the depth of the relief which it covers.
4. Painted enamel, in which a coating of transparent enamel is applied to the substance which forms the design and the reliefs; this substance is applied directly onto the metal, and seen through the transparent enamel, it glitters like a jewel.

Gold and silver were mainly used to make small enamels. As may be noted on this initial, the original of which measures 16 centimetres in height, the enameller began by making small divisions from which to compose the whole, however small, when he desired to achieve a variation in the depth of colour. The piece was set upon a wooden support, to which the plaques of metal, variously shaped according to their position in the design, were nailed. The heads of the nails were then levelled to the surface and after polishing, appeared only as small ornamental points.

Several reasons account for the division of the piece into so many small fragments. Counter-enamelling, in which the reverse side of the plaque is covered with enamel, to prevent any contraction or curling of the metal during firing, was unknown at that time. Moreover, it was necessary to proceed piece by piece, since the duration and intensity of firing differ according to the nature of the enamels being used.

This piece is composed of ten enamelled plaques which were fashioned separately. At the junction of the two curves, the decoration terminates in a lion's head, from the mouth of which a magnificent scroll in simulated relief shoots forth in a double spiral. It is attached to the outline of the letter by the tips of the leaves growing somewhat haphazardly around it.

The artist shaped the two corners of the letter in strong Celtic interlacings which terminate in the head of an animal. In fact, these pieces secure the whole and therefore require greater strength than the others. This explains why the artist employed *cloisonné* in *champlevé*, a technique for which the plaque was necessarily thick so as to resist the effects of firing.

In order to enrich the surface of the metal plaques which make up the body of the letter, the artist employed the technique of *basse-taille*, forming designs inspired by the acanthus leaf.

Fragment nº 6 represents an ornamental clasp in enamelled goldwork of the tenth century. This clasp is repeated at the four corners and in the middle of both sides of the ornamental frame around a page, with the arched part facing inwards. Nº 5, which represents the winged lion of Saint Mark in a quatrefoil medallion of the seventh century, seems to belong to a similar style.

Nº 7. Fragment of painted architecture, Romanesque style, eleventh century. Nº 8 is a floral ornament from the same source. These fragments are taken from a missal written in Latin which belonged to the abbey of Luxeuil, in Franche-Comté.

Only a few folios of this important manuscript are still extant. However, the full-page paintings which adorn it are so exceptionally sumptuous and the workmanship so precise, that this manuscript is considered to be a model of the Romano-Byzantine style and one of the treasures of Christian art.

Following the year 1003, there was a great movement in Europe which could be described as the dawn of a new age, a total renewal. "The world", writes Rodolphe Glaber, a monk of that time, "bestirring itself, cast aside its old age"; and the arts, along with society in general, rose from their lethargy. It is mainly in Italy and France that the traces of this fresh burst of activity are to be found, especially in the building of new churches. For with the exception of the cathedrals and basilicas of the most prosperous abbeys, churches were made of wood, and most of them had either fallen into ruins or had burned down.

Romano-Byzantine art developed particularly in the provinces of France, between the Loire and the Mediterranean, as well as in the regions along the Rhine. The interior architecture of this period is comparable to that of any other great age, as can be seen in the example on the previous page. The designer Flandrin drew his inspiration from illuminations like those in the Luxeuil manuscript to bring this unique aspect to the splendid choir of the church of Saint-Germain-des-Prés.

Displayed above is the complete architectural design of which only a fragment appears in our plate. It is one of the eleven designs containing the ten canons of the Gospel, which are each set in gilded letters on a crimson ground, with magnificent porticos framing them. The columns supporting the capitals are in coloured marble which is in places wholly gilded or painted. In the centre of the main arch is a medallion representing the head and shoulders of an apostle; in this case Simon. On each side of this arch, foliated scrolls support figures representing carpenters, roofers, or, as here, vine-trimmers; or else they support figures of cocks, cranes, swans, eagles holding their prey, and so on, which have a symbolic meaning. The goat which appears in fragment nº 8 belongs to this category.

The basis of Romano-Byzantine architecture is displayed in the twin arcades under a large arch represented in nº 3. A medallion is set in the centre, containing the effigy of Saint Peter holding his keys, and it is adorned on each side with a scroll on which the cock of repudiation is perched. This ornamentation dates from the eighth century. It is the frontispiece to an edition of the four Gospels, which are indicated by the four subdivisions of the main arch. The arch itself can be seen as an image of the rainbow which God places in the clouds, as a token of the "eternal alliance between Him and all the living souls who endow with life all flesh on earth".

This subdivision of the great arch into four parts is that of the portico of the Luxeuil manuscript.

Nº 1

British Museum.

Nº 2

First page of a Gospel of Saint Matthew, which belongs to the library of Stockholm. VIth to IXth century.

Nºs 3 and 4

Gospel belonging to the library of Trèves. VIIIth century.

Nº 5

First page of a Gospel of Saint Mark. British Museum. VIIth century.

Nº 6

Latin missal. Royal Library of Copenhagen. Xth century.

The Missal of Luxeuil belongs to the Bibliothèque Nationale, in Paris.

With the exception of nºs 7 and 8, all the other documents are taken from the magnificent collection published by Westwood.

CELTICO-BYZANTIN.

CELTIC-BYZANTINE.

KELTISCH-BYZANTINISCH

Cottelot lith.

Imp. Firmin-Didot & Cie Paris

MIDDLE AGES.

ORNAMENTATION OF MANUSCRIPTS.

BORDERS AND FLEURETS, VIIITH—XIITH CENTURY.

The corner motifs on this plate represent borders which are placed facing each other on the page, either lengthwise or widthwise. They belong to the secondary Anglo-Saxon style, known as the exfoliated style, which was common to England and Normandy from the ninth to the thirteenth century.

This type of magnificent ornamentation, which is certainly based on Byzantine models, was developed by the Anglo-Saxons in an isolated school confined within the walls of the monasteries of Saint Swithun and New Minster, which are both located in Winchester.

It is claimed that Saint Dunstan, who excelled in the art of illuminating and who was one of the great minds of the tenth-century episcopate, was the founder of this school, the productions of which were characterized by the name *opus anglicum*.

The two manuscripts from which our examples of borders are taken are attributed to Godemann, or to some artist of his school. One is the Benedictional of Archbishop Robert, who was abbot of New Minster and who died Archbishop of Canterbury. The other is the Missal known as the Missal of Robert Champart or Robert the Norman. It, too, belonged to the Archbishop of Canterbury, who brought these two manuscripts over to the monastery of Jumièges, of which he was abbot after his banishment from England, and where he died in 1052 or 1056.

N°s 5 and 6 are taken from the Benedictional, n°s 1, 3 and 7, from the Missal. These two manuscripts belong to the library of Rouen. N°s 2 and 4 are reproductions of studies of the Anglo-Saxon style made by Langlois.

The fleuret, n° 10, belongs to the same style, and is found in the library of Grenoble. Homily, manuscript n° 22.

N° 9 is in a pure Byzantine style dating back to the eigth century. It represents the eagle, the emblem of Saint John the Evangelist according to the miniaturist's tradition laid down by the scholar Alcuin, at the court of Charlemagne. "The eagle", says Alcuin, "is the emblem of John because it ascends on high." This example is taken from the famous Gospels of Charlemagne, transcribed around 781 by Gottschalk, who took no less than seven years to illuminate it. (Bibliothèque Nationale, in Paris.)

N° 8. Fleuret taken from a German manuscript of the twelfth century. (Bibliothèque Nationale, in Paris.)

Bénard lith.

Imp. Firmin-Didot & Cie Paris

CELTIC.

INTERLACINGS AND *DRAKSLINGORS*. ORNAMENTATION OF MANUSCRIPTS FROM THE VIIth TO THE IXth CENTURY.

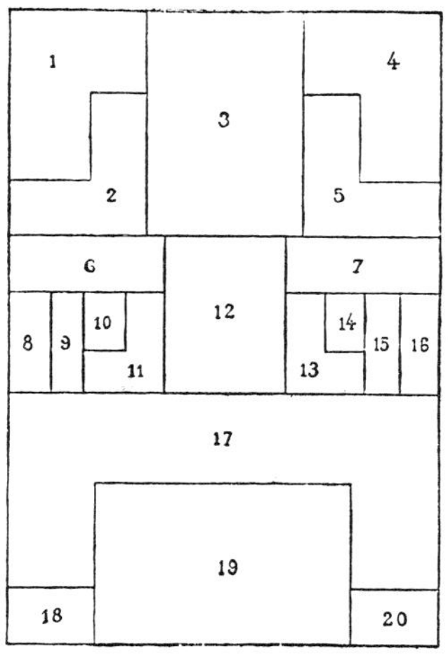

Motifs of the seventh century. Nos 1 and 4, from the Gospel of Saint Matthew and nos 3, 7, 9, 10, 12, 17 and 19, from the Gospels of Durrow. (Trinity Coll., Dublin.) No 6, manuscript from the British Museum.

Examples of the eighth century. Nos 2 and 5, taken from a Gospel of Saint Matthew in Saint Petersburg, which belonged to the abbey of Saint-Germain des Prés. No 8, from the Lindisfarne Gospels.

The ninth century is represented by nos 11 and 13, from the Gospels of Mac Durnan, a manuscript bearing the date 850 (Lambeth Palace Library), and by nos 15, 16, 18 and 20, taken from the manuscripts of the library of Saint Gall.

The *drakslingors* or "dragons", whose intricate patterns compose so fine a decoration on runic stones, are also found on metal objects from the island of Gotland, which dates back to the time of the Vikings.

English critics, who consider the Celtic style to be wholly the product of their own national genius, refer to it as the Anglo-Saxon style, although it was mastered superlatively well by the Irish, who are Celts. The Swedes and the Danes refer to it as the Celtico-Scandinavian style. We shall merely retain the name Celtic.

Our plate distinguished by the symbol of the *weathercock* displays examples of the development of this style, which sometimes represents human figures. Very often only the heads of birds, of serpents or of quadrupeds were used to terminate the interplay of lines. We would simply mention here that the purest examples of this style are also the oldest, since they date from the seventh century. They precede all Byzantine influence, thus bearing witness to the originality of the style.

Chataignon, lith.

Imp. Firmin Didot & Cie. Paris

MIDDLE AGES.

CELTICO-SCANDINAVIAN ORNAMENTATION FROM THE VIIth TO THE IXth CENTURY.

EPIGRAPHIC DOCUMENTS.

N° 1.

Section of the first page of the Gospel of Saint Matthew, found in the *Golden Book* of the library of Stockholm, of the seventh or eighth century.

The text of this first page, following a custom which was then widespread, is written in majuscule roman letters. It begins with a monogram in Greek letters; the chi X is the first letter of the word ΧΡΙΣΤΟΣ, whence the designation *christianus* originated. This initial, usually accompanied by the rho P and the iota I, is the most ancient abridged or mysterious designation of the name of Jesus Christ.

The details of ornamentation on this monogram and those on the first line of the text are most remarkably rich and fine. The artist employed all the possibilities of the Scandinavian style, avoiding monotony by varying the details.

N° 2.

Another monogram of Christ in Greek letters, with an elongated *Chi*. First page of the text of a Gospel of Saint Matthew from the library of Saint Gall, eighth or ninth century.

Examples of interlaced dragons, the drakslingors, of which the runic stones present such fine specimens, are displayed here, as well as combinations of meanders arranged diagonally. Patterns of dots are often employed in this style and they are generally placed one by one on narrow dividing bands. When they form the whole decoration of a letter, as on the PI, they may be placed three by three.

Motifs n°s 7, 8 and 9, taken from the same manuscript, are further examples of what has been said about this style.

N°s 3, 4, 5 and 6.

The initial Q, the letter O, the motif in a spiral and the border in regular interlacings, are examples from the seventh century. (Gospels of Durrow, Trinity Coll., Dublin.)

All these examples are taken from the great work of Westwood: *Fac-Similes of the Miniatures and Ornaments of Anglo-Saxon and Irish Manuscripts.*

Cottelot, lith. Imp. Firmin-Didot & Cie Paris.

MIDDLE AGES.

ORNAMENTATION OF MANUSCRIPTS. VIIIth, IXth, Xth CENTURIES.

GALLO-FRANKISH AND ANGLO-SAXON SCHOOLS.

Although the Empire of Charlemagne did not last until the tenth century, the period comprising the VIIIth, IXth and Xth centuries is referred to as the Carolingian epoch. However, it was during the reign of Charlemagne that an important literary renewal occurred. This was also reflected in the arts in general, which in consequence of the turmoil resulting from the partition of the Empire in the second part of the ninth century, were not able to resume their progress until the eleventh century.

In northern Europe, the illumination of manuscripts seems to have originated towards the seventh century, under the influence of Anglo-Saxon and English missionaries who had visited the East. At the same time, another movement closer to the neo-Greek style originated in the southern part of Europe and spread northwards, creating the Lombard, German and Visigothic sub-groups, and particularly the Gallo-Frankish school in central France, which scholars date from 700 to 950.

The documents on the accompanying plate exemplify the fusion between the Greco-Byzantine style and interlacing of the Celtic style. All the manuscripts in which these examples are found appear to predate the year 1000. They are listed below in chronological order, as assigned to them by archeologists.

N° 8.

(Placed within the ornamental frame n° 7) The words *In Principio*, with an ornamented initial, from the beginning of the Gospel of Saint John, are taken from a book of Gospels dating from the eighth or ninth century which belonged to the church of Saint-Pierre, at Liège. The ornamentation of the initials of this manuscript are splendid specimens of Carolingian art, although they are only draught designs. The original of the first initial measures 23 centimetres. It has been photographically reduced.

N° 3.

Initial based on the kind of *drakslingors* engraved on Celtico-Scandinavian runic stones. Ninth century. Taken from a psalter belonging to Cambridge University.

N° 7.

Border taken from the Gospels of the Emperor Lothair, who died in 855. Manuscript written and illuminated for this sovereign in the royal Abbey of Saint-Martin, in Tours. Gallo-Frankish school. (Bibliothèque Nationale, in Paris.)

N° 2.

Upper part of a page border which represents the Saviour. Tenth-century Gospels. Byzantine elements, Anglo-Saxon school. (Cambridge University.)

N° 4.

Border of a page composed of similar elements, treated with great delicacy, tenth century; part of a donation made by King Edgar to the Cathedral of Winchester, in 966. (British Museum.)

N° 5.

Initial representing the *Word made flesh* and forming the first letter of the *In Principio* at the beginning of the Gospel of Saint John. Combination of Celtic and Byzantine styles. Tenth century. (Public Library of Bologna.)

N° 1.

Initial of the *Beatus* which begins the Psalms of David. Around the year 1000. Celtic ornamentation, Byzantine figures. Anglo-Saxon Latin psalter. (Public Library of Bologna.)

N° 6.

Running border from the same source.

With the exception of n°s 7 and 8, all these documents are taken from the work of Westwood on the Anglo-Saxon style.

MIDDLE-AGES — MOYEN-AGE — MITTEL-ALTER

Lestel, lith.

Imp. Firmin-Didot & Cie, Paris

MIDDLE AGES.

MOSAICS AND PAINTINGS. GALLO-ROMAN AND ROMANESQUE EPOCHS.

N°s 9 and 13.

Gallo-Roman mosaics discovered in 1842 at Bielle, in the valley of Ossau (Basses-Pyrénées), which are today almost entirely destroyed.

The style of these decorations is essentially Roman. The workmanship of the small cubes of stone, marble and brick, is of great perfection. The cubes are inlaid in a white cement forming a division between all these minute elements, which thereby mitigates all the tones, and produces a harmonious relationship between the colours without lessening the strength of the design.

N°s 7 and 11.

Mosaics from Pondoly, near Jurançon (Basses-Pyrénées). They are taken from thermal baths which offer a remarkable example of Gallo-Roman art. These mosaics, which were discovered in 1802, are now entirely destroyed.

N° 3.

Border forming part of a fragment which is the sole vestige of a Gallo-Roman mosaic. The mosaic, set on pink cement, measured fifteen square metres and was discovered in 1860, in the cemetery of Taron (Basses-Pyrénées). This magnificent border, the original of which no longer exists, combines fine workmanship with an excellent design.

N°s 2 and 5.

Fragment and repeated motif of the Romanesque epoch, twelfth century, church of Sordes (Landes). The construction of this church dates back to the end of the eleventh century. Only its apses are still extant, in which the mosaics are found. Although the Byzantine style prevails in these vestiges, the mosaics are generally seen as marking a transition to the Romanesque style.

N[os] 1, 4, 6, 8 and 10.

Borders and a fleuret, painted in the Bible of Saint-Martial of Limoges, which dates from the Franco-Romanesque period (950 to 1200).

N° 12.

Fleuret, taken from the Bible of Grenoble, MS n° 650. Twelfth century, Franco-Romanesque.

The mosaics are reproduced from the drawings displayed at the exhibition organized by the Union centrale des arts décoratifs in 1876.

MOYEN-AGE

MIDDLE-AGES | MITTEL-ALTER

Guesnu, lith. Imp. Firmin Didot & Cie, Paris

MIDDLE AGES.

GALLO-ROMAN AND ROMANESQUE MOSAICS.

N°s 4 and 5.

Mosaics from Pondoly, near Jurançon (Basses-Pyrénées). Discovered in Gallo-Roman thermal baths.

N°s 1, 2, 3 and 6.

Mosaics from the church of Sordes (Landes). These mosaics seem to indicate the transition from the Byzantine style, which predominates, to the Romanesque style. The elongated figures of animals in the rosette are heraldic in nature.

Reproduced from the drawings exhibited by the Union centrale des arts décoratifs in 1876.

1 2 3 4 5 6

Lestel, lith. Imp. Firmin-Didot & Cie, Paris

MIDDLE-AGES.

BAS-RELIEFS, IRONWORK AND PAINTED ORNAMENTATION.

FRENCH SCHOOLS FROM THE XITH TO THE XIVTH CENTURY.

These ornaments are taken from the catalogue of the exhibit organized by the Union centrale des arts décoratifs in 1876, at the Palace of the Champs-Elysées.

Provençal School.

N°s 1 and 2.

Bas-reliefs of the Carolingian era, from the cathedral of Viviers (Ardèche). The chapel on the first floor of this church is topped by a cupola by Salardus. Parts of this church are adorned with finely sculptured friezes, scrolls, and figures of animals.

School of Poitou.

The principle of this form of ornamentation is still the antique palmette.

N°s 3 and 4.

Door fittings from the church of Neuvy Sainte-Sépulcre (Indre). This eleventh-century church has a circular structure, in imitation of the Holy Sepulchre. Drawings from Viollet-le-Duc, who directed the restoration of this edifice.

N°s 5, 6 and 7.

Paintings from the church of the old priory of Saint-Désiré (Allier). The apse dates from the end of the eleventh century, the nave from the thirteenth century. Very remarkable crypt of the ninth or tenth century.

Burgundian School.

N°s 8 and 9.

Carved wood, uprights of a door, from the old abbey of Charlieu (Loire), eleventh or twelfth century. Today only the following parts of the church survive: the magnificent portico, one of the finest specimens of Burgundian Romanesque architecture; part of the cloisters, which were rebuilt in the fifteenth century; and the building formerly occupied by the prior.

N° 8 is a pearled meander, n° 9 is a double undulating ribbon.

Mural Paintings.

The catalogue does not refer mural paintings to specific schools, as these forms of decoration do not bear sufficiently close relationship to the architecture of the monuments.

N°s 10 and 11.

Mural paintings from the chapel of Liget (Indre-et-Loire). These paintings on pillars are here illustrated in their basic form, though they may be readily expanded to indicate their full expression. They date from the middle of the twelfth century. The six patterns with which this chapel is adorned are placed between the seven windows of the circular part of the monument, and cover the whole height of these windows.

N° 12.

Mural painting from the church of Saint-Philibert of Tournus (Saône-et-Loire); thirteenth and fourteenth centuries.

MIDDLE AGES. MOYEN-AGE. MITTEL ALTER.

Waret, del. Imp. Firmin Didot & Cie Paris

MIDDLE AGES.

PAINTED ORNAMENTATIONS.

FRENCH SCHOOLS FROM THE XITH TO THE XIVTH CENTURIES.

These documents form a continuation to those of the plate distinguished by the symbol of the *shako*. They are taken from the catalogue of the same exhibition.

Norman School.

N[os] 1, 2, 3, 4, 5, 6 and 7.

Paintings from the former abbey of Hambye (Manche), which dates back to the year 1145. The church seems to have been erected in the thirteenth century. N° 5 is a horizontal frieze, all the other specimens are vault friezes.

School of the Ile-de-France.

N[os] 8 and 9.

Paintings from the first half of the thirteenth century, from the church of the former abbey of Saint-Jean aux Bois (Oise).

N[os] 10 and 11.

Paintings from the Sainte-Chapelle of Paris, which was erected under the reign of Saint Louis, by Pierre de Montereau, 1242–1247. In the fifteenth century, under Charles VII, certain parts of the edifice were modified. In the nineteenth century, a restoration was undertaken by Duban and Lassus, and completed by Boeswillwald. Drawings by the latter, Viollet-le-Duc and Steinheil. The yellow colour on these details is gold in the originals.

Mural Paintings.

We would repeat here that the catalogue does not include mural paintings, as they are not related closely enough to the different schools.

N° 12.

Frieze painting from the church of Saint-Jean, at Poitiers (Vienne). This church, which is often referred to as a Temple, because its façade is adorned with a pediment in the proportions of Antiquity, is the former baptistry of the town. It apparently dates from the sixth century. The meander has a definitely ancient character.

N° 13.

Painting from the Cathedral of Clermont (Puy-de-Dôme). XIVth century.

N°s 14, 15 and 16.

Paintings from the church of Saint-Philibert of Tournus (Saône-et-Loire), thirteenth and fourteenth centuries. We possess no historical details about this monument. As for the paintings, in which one finds the ancient acanthus leaf, they almost seem to herald the Renaissance.

Waret del. Imp. Firmin Didot & Cie. Paris

MIDDLE AGES.

MOSAICS IN COLOURED PASTES, ENAMELLED GLASS, AND MARBLE. PAINTED ENAMEL *EN RÉSILLE SUR VERRE.*

IXTH—XIIITH CENTURIES.

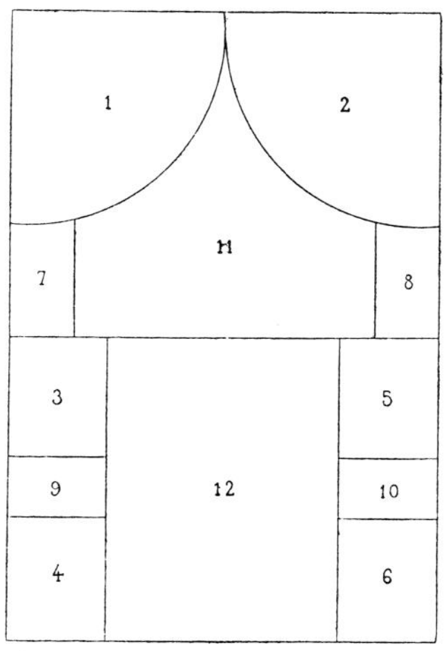

With the exception of the large initial, these documents are from Saint Mark's in Venice, the erection of which began in 976 and was completed in 1071. Naturally, many details postdate the year of completion. The architecture and its ornamentation, which date from the ninth to the twelfth century, belong to the second period of Byzantine art; a third period resulted from the Venetian conquests.

The two rosettes, n°s 1 and 2, represent the most sumptuous decoration of polychrome Byzantine architecture. The use of coloured pastes, of enamelled glass on a golden ground, and the arrangement of the materials, create the illusion that the scrolls are standing out in relief. Fashioned in this manner, a decoration of this type appears to take on the aspect of a piece of jewellery.

Borders, with vertical or horizontal patterns, as shown in n°s 7, 8, 9 and 10, which are found everywhere on the inner walls of the monument, were not treated with the same luxury. Our examples are made of glass, painted or inlaid with enamel, the transparency of the grounds imparting a sense of movement to them.

The marble mosaics shown in n°s 3, 4, 5, 6 and 11 are all motifs from pavements, the composition of which is based on the same principle as marquetry, that is to say in a more rigid style. This probably contributes to their appearing more ancient than the other mosaics.

N° 12 is a painting on a manuscript dating from the twelfth or the early thirteenth century. The original, a bible in two volumes, the Old and the New Testament, is at the British Museum (n°s 2798 and 2799).

Bénard, lith. Imp. Firmin-Didot & Cie Paris

MIDDLE AGES.

ORNAMENTATION OF MANUSCRIPTS. VIIIth–XIIIth CENTURIES.

SCROLLWORK, EMBLEMATIC DECORATION.

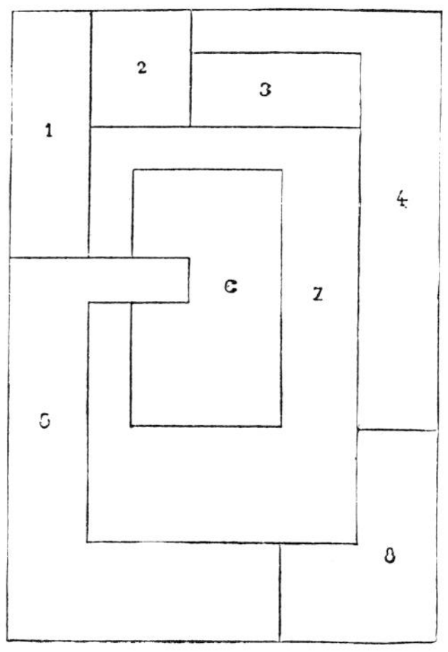

N° 3.

Motif formed with interlacing in the Celtic style. Taken from the Gospels of Charlemagne, a manuscript of the eighth century from the former monastery and priory of Saint-Martin-des-Champs, in Paris. Gallo-Frankish school, 700 to 950. (Bibliothèque Nationale.)

E, initial letter taken from a German manuscript of the second part of the eleventh century. Latin Gospels written for the abbey of Luxeuil, in Franche-Comté. (Bibliothèque Nationale.)

N°s 1 and 4.

Fragments of a page border, from a manuscript of the Harleian library, n° 2, 800, at the British Museum. These splendid examples of late twelfth-century work are found in the first part of a *Lives of the Saints* in three volumes. The colours are of great simplicity, covering only the grounds, in accordance with the ironwork after which they were modelled. This manuscript may have been illuminated for the monastery of Arrinstein, near Koblentz.

N°s 5 and 7.

Borders of pages, the motifs of which were taken from another manuscript of the Haleian library in the British Museum, a bible in two volumes, n°s 2798–2799, with the same origins as n°s 1 and 4. These two decorations have a symbolic value in addition to the beauty of their scrollwork. N° 7 is the ornamental framing of the page on which the prophecies of Jeremiah begin. On the strip of parchment held by the prophet, the original presents the inscription *Verba Jeremie*, "the words of Jeremiah". At the very beginning of the famous Lamentations, God promises Jeremiah to render him as firm as an iron column or a bronze wall in the face of his enemies. The artist has expressed this in the erect attitude of the prophet, who treads a dragon under foot. With ornamental foliage shooting forth from its mouth, the painter has fashioned the dragon into a splendid decorative motif.

Fragment n° 5 is taken from a page of the Fourth Book of Kings, in the same volume. The prophesying figure is probably Elijah, whose words are represented by the abundant scrolls which coil out of his mouth.

N° 6.

Fragments of a page border. This twelfth-century motif is taken from the missal which belonged to the Abbey of Saint-Maur-les-Fossés, in the diocese of Paris.

N° 8.

Border motif taken from the Missal of Saint-Denis, of the thirteenth century. These two examples represent the *School of Paris* (Paris, Saint-Denis, Meaux and Chartres) which came under Oriental influences during the first Gothic period, from 1200 to 1300.

Taillefer, lith. Imp. Firmin Didot & Cie, Paris

MIDDLE AGES.

PAINTINGS ON MANUSCRIPTS, VIIIth–XIIth CENTURIES.

SCROLLS, CORNERS, BORDERS, ETC.

According to Viollet-le-Duc, the first notions of art in Western Europe spread from Gaul, the territory between the Loire and the Rhine, to the other nations, including Italy, from the ninth to the twelfth century, "notwithstanding the objections of those for whom Western arts necessarily originated in Italy from the time of the Roman Empire". (*Entretiens sur l'architecture*, page 202.) The splendid fragments from the school of Canterbury in our plate confirm this assertion.

According to the classification of the different schools of illumination, established by Sylvestre, Champollion-Figeac, Denis, Viel-Castel and Bastard, the Franco-Saxon school arose around 800, from a fusion of the Southern and the Anglo-Saxon schools.

During the Romanesque period, and under Byzantine influence, there were two schools, the Franco-Romanesque school, from 950 to 1200, and the German-Romanesque from 1000 to 1200; the first Gothic style dating only from 1240.

We shall follow chronological order as far as possible in the list below.

N° 16.

Taken from the Bible known as the Bible of Lothair. — Bibliothèque Nationale, 750–800 (Gallo-Frankish school).

N°s 15, 21, 30.

Latin manuscript, n° 269. — Bibl. Nat., 900–950.

N°s 6 and 7.

Latin manuscript, n° 8878. — Bibl. Nat., 980.

N°s 1 and 4.

Latin manuscript, n° 278. — Bibl. Nat., 1100 (Greco-Lombard).

N°s 8 and 10.

Latin manuscript, n° 8873. — Bibl. Nat., 1100.

N°s 9, 11, 17, 18, 19, 20, 21, 23, 24, 25, 26, 27, 28, 29, 31, 32, 33

(n°s 17 and 23 go together, n° 17 ending the motif.) Biblia sacra in three vols. — Library of Sainte-Geneviève, 1150 (Greco-English).

This manuscript, transcribed by Manierus of Canterbury, one of the masters of that school, is regarded as a rare and precious example of the Greco-Saxon style of that period. Its decorations bear a certain relationship to those of the famous manuscript of Æthelgar, which forms part of the public library of Rouen. N°s 22, 23, 17 and 29 present new and unknown shapes, as does n° 25, which is of Byzantine expression, thoroughly modified by Saxon genius.

N°s 2, 5 and 3.

Latin manuscript, n° 8959. — Bibl. Nat., 1150.

N°s 12, 13 and 14.

Manuscript n° 212. — Bibl. Nat., 1190 (French).

MOYEN-ÂGE

MIDDLE AGES　　　　MITTEL ALTER

Bénard lith.　　　　Imp. Firmin Didot & Cie Paris

MIDDLE-AGES.

DECORATION ON FABRICS OF GRECO-SYRIAN CHARACTER.

HISTORICAL OUTLINE.

1 2

3 4

The importation into the West of Oriental fabrics, the finest of which came essentially from Constantinople, Jerusalem, and several Greek towns, goes back to the early Middle Ages, and for centuries their features appear to have remained identical. Until the end of the thirteenth century, the products of the Western manufactories were, with few exceptions, imitations of the Greek, the Persian or the Egyptian styles. So that the thick silk cloths of the fourteenth century are decorated in a style belonging to previous epochs.

N°s 1 and 2 are taken from the portfolio left by Prisse d'Avennes. N° 2 is the fragment of a border with a repeated design, each section being adorned alternately with an eagle or a lion. It is an orphrey of eminently Byzantine character, although there is no annotation to indicate the origin.

N° 1 is the border and the ground decoration of a chasuble. This part-coloured fabric of crimson and violet, which presents the richest of aspects in accordance with Byzantine opulence, is one of the finest existing specimens of designs woven in the weft. The animals facing each other in the design belong to the Syrian tradition, whilst the dividing meanders bordered with small running patterns are in keeping with the Greek style. Lastly the separate border recalls the finest of Moorish meanders.

N° 3 is found amongst the ornaments of Aix-la-Chapelle. The decoration clearly expresses the sacerdotal destination of the fabric and its Christian character, whilst remaining close to certain styles of pagan times. The stem with coiled ends represents the pastor's crosier, while the vase is the Greek *krossos*, a container used for water or funerary ashes. The three eucharistic hosts which appear over each of these vases confirm with great clarity the nature of the decoration, their triple image recalling the mystery of the Trinity. Lastly, the design in the shape of a cross set in the central intervals completes the Christian symbolism. The red ground of the fabric, a prerogative of those of the highest rank, helped to raise pontiffs to the level of sovereigns.

N° 4. Silk fabrics of various colours mingled with gold and even pearls, seem for a long time to have been reserved for priestly vestments. The present fabric appears to be one of those samites worn by knights over their coats of mail, towards the end of the twelfth century. The proportion of the design corresponded to its use, as it is reduced here only by half. In the manner in which the pairs of birds and foxes are placed in symmetrical opposition, it exhibits the typical arrangement which Viollet-le-Duc pointed out as characterizing the ancient Oriental tradition.

1 2 3 4 5

Taillefer, lith.

Imp. Firmin Didot & Cie Paris

ROMANO-BYZANTINE.

ENAMELLED AND HARD STONE MOSAICS. PAVEMENTS AND FACINGS.

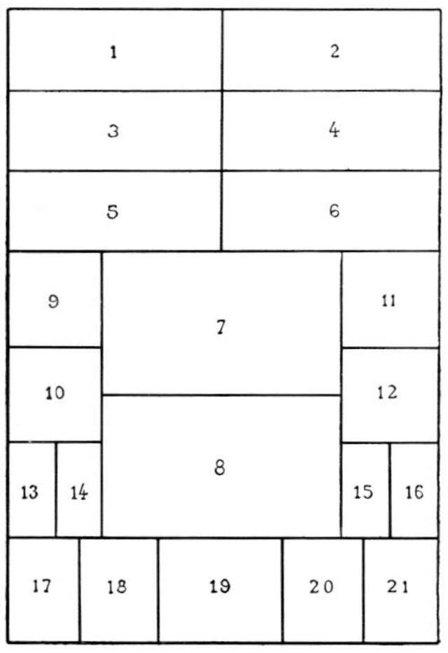

Nos 10, 15, 16, 18 and 20. Fragments of the pavement of the basilica of Santa Maria in Cosmedin, in Rome (in Greek *cosmedin* signifies ornament). The ornamented Saint Mary owes its appellation to the magnificence with which, in 728, Pope Hadrian I had it decorated. The style of this pavement, a mosaic made of porphyry and precious marble, which covers the whole surface of the nave, is related to the century of that pontiff.

Nos 9, 11, 12, 13, 14, 17, 19 and 21. Mosaics of a similar style, found in the choir of the church of Saint-Benoît-sur-Loire (Loiret). The rarest sorts of marble, jasper, porphyry and ophite, which were brought over from Italy in the sixteenth century, are employed in them.

Nos 1, 2, 3, 4, 5, 6, 7 and 8. Enamelled mosaics from the Palatine chapel in Palermo, which dates from the first part of the twelfth century, and examples from the church of Santa Cesarea, in Rome.

Only in Italy is it possible to find such fine decoration, in which the monumental beauty and the deep colours of porphyry set off the contrasting gold and varied tones of the enamel. This type of mosaic was very difficult to fashion, as the encrustation of marble is a laborious process, and the small dimensions of the geometrical designs thus formed required extreme precision. This style was very successful in the twelfth, thirteenth and fourteenth centuries, particularly within the Roman states. For the most part they were manufactured in cloisters by monks. In the eleventh century, most of the abbots of great monasteries in Italy, especially Didier, abbot of Monte Cassino, founded mosaic schools in their religious institutions.

This mosaic-work, inlaid according to a geometric arrangement, gave rise to a similar type of marquetry made of wood or ivory for the adornment of small objects. This marquetry was so extremely fine, that, because wood fibres could not be cut into pieces as exiguous as required, eventually the work was confined to ivory previously tinged with green or with any other lasting colour.

Schmidt lith.

Imp. Firmin-Didot & Cie. Paris

MIDDLE AGES.

COLOURED STAINED GLASS OF THE XIIth, XIIIth AND XIVth CENTURIES.

THE OGIVAL WINDOW DECORATED WITH ORNAMENTAL FOLIAGE.

JEWELLERY IN ARCHITECTURE.

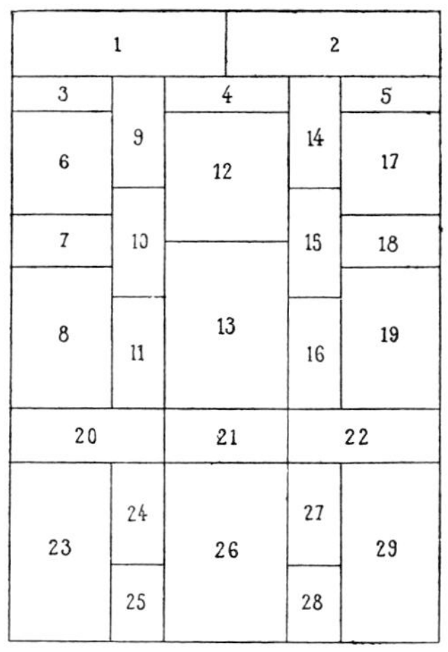

Nos 1 and 2.

Borders. Cathedral of Angers.

Nos 3, 9, 14, 15, 16, 24, 27 and 28.

Cathedral of Bourges.

Nos 23 and 29.

Grounds. Same origin.

Nos 5, 7 and 18.

Borders and edging. Cathedral of Chartres.

Nos 10 and 11.

Borders. Saint-Rémi of Reims.

No 6.

Ground. Same origin.

Nos 20 and 22.

Borders. Cathedral of Sens.

Nos 12, 13, 17 and 26.

Grounds. Same origin.

No 25.

Border. Cathedral of Soissons.

Nos 4 and 21.

Border and edging. Cathedral of Strasbourg.

No 8.

Ground. Cathedral of Reims.

No 19.

Ground. Chapter-house of Salisbury.

In the twelfth, thirteenth and fourteenth centuries, stained glass windows were part and parcel of the construction and served no other purpose but to enhance the effect produced by the work of the architect. Painting on glass was not yet a separate art, as it became in the fifteenth century.

The ornamentation of the stained glass window consists of two distinct elements, the borders and the main part of the window, the functions of which differ greatly.

The border, which follows the exact shape of the ogive, is an adornment the function of which is not to light, but to underscore the forms of the architecture. Its character was modelled after the supple piping cord, decorated with enamelled metalwork, fixed upon a silk or velvet ground, which was used on garments of that time. The glass was dyed in large pieces in uniform colours, generally blue and red, sometimes green, and then frosted on one side to lessen their luminosity. Often the layer of glass was doubled to obtain a relief, or covered with paint to render it relatively opaque, in order to set off the designs by a dark ground. The edging or *bordurette* was usually decorated with a running pattern; it was an extension of the border, which was always placed on the inner side of the window.

The main part of the window, on the other hand, was decorated in such a way as to admit light. The type of glass-work which let in a measured amount of daylight was modelled after white silk fabric, damasked with small designs in an Oriental style (nº 23). It is on this ground that the features of a coloured decoration were set, representing embroidered or inlaid motifs, sometimes enriched with pearls and scallops. In consequence, the more or less transparent ornamentation had the aspect of woven openwork.

It was probably the architect who indicated the width to be given to the borders, according to the nature of the stone construction, and who completed the interior aspect of the edifice with these rich, vigorous and sparkling margins. Indeed, the structure of the mullions dividing the windows would have seemed too thin and frail without the fine double border.

The possibilities of these more or less Byzantine styles really depended on the variety of combinations the artist drew from them. The artist who traced the cartoons which the artisan copied, had to comply with the constraints of the craft, facilitating the work of the glass cutter. For, generally speaking, a stained-glass window is simply a big jig-saw puzzle, composed of pieces of glass. These pieces of glass were either coloured by dyeing in large pieces or painted with a brush which traced in grey, brown or black the inner details of the ornamentation, then vitrified by firing. When each of these fragments of various dimensions and shapes were completed, they were assembled between the lead wires which outline the motifs. The whole structure was then set into a general metallic framework.

There were two sorts of craftsmen: those who did the work of a painter whilst modelling the ornamentation of the border; and those who dealt with the less complicated and generally larger fragments of the central part of the window. The latter were generally less qualified workers, for whom, in order to guide them more carefully, the artist traced with ruler and compass the main outlines of the cartoons. However, despite the efforts of the artist to ease their work, it was still particularly laborious, as the use of diamond to cut glass was not discovered until the sixteenth century.

Nevertheless, the activity of the stained-glass artists seems not to have been impeded by the various difficulties of the art, for the work they produced, along with that of artists and craftsmen of other branches of craft work, was immense. Without the testimony of several contemporaries, it would be quite impossible for us to understand how a sufficient number of workers were found to build within so short a time all those imposing religious constructions which have given Europe its most powerful architectural achievement through their magnificent exteriors and interiors.

The movement to build cathedrals was especially vigorous during the times of the Crusades, which merely one example will suffice to illustrate: as early as the eleventh century, the number of workers employed in the construction of the Cathedral of Strasburg amounted to one hundred thousand.

These crowds erected temples whose luxury expressed the might of the divine protector from whom assistance was being sought. Both noblemen and bondsmen regarded God as inseparable from wealth, which confers power, and in this respect nothing was spared to render the monument as eloquent as possible. Hence, the magnificent cathedral was sculptured and painted in many ways and adorned with that marvel of marvels, the coloured enamel of stained glass-work. The great church was made to appear like a gigantic Ark, sailing in the spiritual half-light of the stained glass, and offering shelter to the congregations of the Middle Ages.

Bauer lith. Imp. Firmin Didot & Cie. Paris

MIDDLE-AGES.

EUROPEAN BROCADES OF ORIENTAL CHARACTER, FROM PAINTINGS.

N° 1.

This fragment represents a brocaded silk fabric of the fifteenth century, taken from a painting by Marziale Marco, in the Contarini Gallery, in Venice.

The ground is in white satin, and the characteristics of the decoration are both Persian and Indian. The ramifications recall the ingenious combinations of Persian tilework, and the flora belong mostly to the Indian style. This decoration is one of the most charming types of brocaded silk fabrics, known during the Middle Ages as the *Saracen* genre. While the workmanship of this brocade is European, its Oriental model probably underwent few modifications after it was supplied to the Venetian manufactories, which then worked for the whole of Europe.

N° 3

From a painting by Giottino at the Uffizi in Florence; it is a sacerdotal fabric of Byzantine character. Silvered material spangled with gold and brocaded with red and black velvet; the letters are in gold. This inscription is typical. ΙΧΟΥΣ means "fish" in Greek. The fish was the symbolic representation of the Lord; it was the password of the first Christians. The Greek word for fish is believed to have provided the five initial letters of the five words signifying "Jesus Christ", "son of God", and "Saviour". The palms which divide this decoration have an emblematic meaning as well, for the palm was the reward for whoever triumphed over all trials of faithfulness to God. Sacerdotal vestments often bear inscriptions in Latin, and, more rarely, in Greek.

N°s 2 and 4

From a painting by primitives of the Academy of Florence. These examples are from the first part of the fifteenth century.

One of these fragments is red velvet spangled with gold, and its decoration consists of florets. The other is green velvet spangled with gold, in which the plant and the animal world are combined to form a repeating pattern. The Oriental and Byzantine influences are still quite obvious, although the style belongs to a period of transition. Until the middle of the fourtenth century, in all the paintings and frescoes in which fabrics are represented, the Byzantine style always appears in the shape of geometric ornaments symmetrically arranged, such as stars, florets, rhombs, and so on. Almost always, the predominating colour apart from gold is poppy red, or light bright green (Veronese green). In our example the movement imparted to the cocks is worthy of notice as it suggests the emergence of a taste for reality. This fragment, n° 4, belongs to a dress. In the Christian symbolism used by the painters of the Roman catacombs, two cocks face to face are the allegory of struggle and martyrdom.

1

2

3

Brandin, lith.

Imp. Firmin-Didot & Cie Paris

MIDDLE AGES.

RUNNING ORNAMENTATION TREATED IN MONOCHROME, FROM THE XIIth TO THE XVth CENTURY.

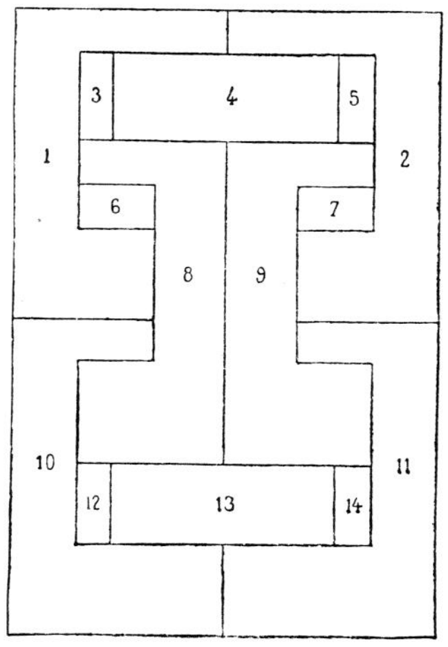

N° 4.

This form of ornamentation can be seen on many works of art from the time of Saint-Louis. Its similarity with the ironwork which adorns the doors of Notre Dame of Paris is striking. For at that time, the school of Paris was especially influenced by Oriental models. Indeed, when the crusaders arrived in the Orient they discovered a fully developed style. The taste for these rich foliated scrolls became predominant in Europe, where craftsmen such as Biscornette, who forged the ironwork on the doors of the Cathedral of Paris, treated this style with the skill of the true master.

Nos 6 and 7.

Examples of one of the types of manuscript ornamentation in use in France from 1150 to 1200, during the final period of the French Romanesque style. Ms. n° 41, Public Library of Grenoble.

Nos 1 and 2.

Margins from a Latin bible of the fourteenth century. Monochrome painting, in silver and red. Conventional plants and fantastic animals. Ms. n° 53, Public Library of Lyon.

N° 13.

This monochrome was painted in Italy, probably in Florence, around 1400. It is taken from a Latin breviary which belonged to the Azzini family. This manuscript is part of the Bibliothèque du Palais des Arts, in Lyon.

N° 11.

Very widespread type of marginal decoration of the fourteenth and early part of the fifteenth centuries. The *Manipulus florum*, from which this motif is taken, was painted in France around 1420. Ms. 251, Public Library in Lyon.

Nos 3, 5, 12 and 14.

Motifs of plants from the frescos and sculptures of the former abbey of the church of Saint-Antoine de Viennois (Isère); fifteenth century.

N° 10.

This example of an ornamentation representing the skeleton of a tree devoid of foliage, which nevertheless produces a most harmonious decoration, is taken from a manuscript known as the *Pontifical of Camille de Neufville*. It was painted in the fifteenth century. N° 89, Public Library of Lyon.

Nos 8 and 9.

These splendid scrolls are examples of one of the styles of manuscript ornamentation used in Italy towards the end of the fifteenth century. Ms. 723, Public Library of Lyon.

Chataignon, lith. Imp. Firmin-Didot & Cie Paris

MIDDLE AGES.

ENAMEL *EN RÉSILLE SUR VERRE*, FROM PAINTINGS ON ITALIAN MANUSCRIPTS.

A painting of the tenth century has shed considerable light on the different techniques of enamelled goldwork of the early Middle Ages, so few examples of which are still extant. The goldsmith was able to combine various techniques in a single piece: plane enamel, transparent or opaque, inlaid in the *cloisonnés en champlevé*, transparent enamel encrusted in the intaglio-work, and painted enamels covered with transparent enamels. (See the *Celtico-Byzantine* plate identified by the symbol of the *hinge*.)

Our Italian illuminations date from the fifteenth century, and therefore make it possible to assign a date to enamel *en résille sur verre*, by indicating who the true inventors of this new technique were. They also exhibit the style of ornamentation employed by the enamellers, who were all craftsmen as well, in compliance with the customs of the Middle Ages.

The technique of enamelling *en résille sur verre* is as follows. Incisions are made on a colourless crystal plaque, which are lined with gold and packed with enamel. Firing at a specific temperature bonds the enamel to the glass and gold; the crystal is then polished so as to level the surface. Lastly, the piece is completed by fixing crimson, green or blue rectangular pieces of foil on the other side of the plaque.

The breadth of the style of these ornamentations *en résille* recalls the Byzantine works of the twelfth century. (See n°s 2, 3, 5, 6, 7, 8, 9, 11, 12 and 13.) In order to enhance the movement of the scrollwork, the grounds, most of which are speckled with gold, vary in intensity as well as in tone. The scroll itself changes colour as it unfurls, turning pink on blue or green grounds, or blue on crimson grounds, and so forth. This use of a series of colours on a single stem is consistent with the general rules of certain optical illusions, and particularly with the analysis of pure colours in opposition, or complementary colours.

N°s 1, 3, 5, 6, 7, 8, 9, 11, 12 and 13 are taken from the margins of the "Little Prayer-Book of the Virgin", which belongs to the convent of Santa Maria Magdalena, in Siena. Manuscript from the fifteenth century.

N°s 2, 4 and 10 are taken from the "Book of the Sisterhood of Saint Catherine", library of Siena. The arms on the medallion of n° 4 are those of the town of Siena.

Spiegel, lith. Imp. Firmin-Didot & Cie. Paris

MIDDLE AGES.

PAINTED AND GILDED WOODWORK OF THE XVth CENTURY. ROSES AND PANELS.

These examples are taken from pieces of furniture, the undulating decorations of which are typical of the Flamboyant Gothic style (see the two panels). The tracery of that time generally has a prismatic shape, with narrow and projecting edges. The same rules which guided the Gothic ornamentalist in large-scale constructions are also found in the carved woodwork of furniture. It is therefore possible to study the style from these examples of woodwork, the sizes of which did not have to be greatly reduced in order to fit our plate.

The most common type of decoration of the Flamboyant epoch consists of blank tracery resembling the inner divisions of Gothic windows.

These decorative panels were coloured in order to strengthen the illusion of openwork, which most of the time was only simulated.

These roses are imitations of the rose-window. Those of the fifteenth century elude generic description by the variety of combinations they offer, in which curvilinear trefoils and quatrefoils, broken lines, and so on, form intricate and symmetrical patterns.

In our museums, such as the Cluny Museum, it is possible to find several examples of furniture decoration from the fifteenth century. Their paint and gilding have been preserved from the destruction caused by the habit of polishing furniture. The painted colours are especially important as they set off the tracery of the decoration.

Brandin, lith. Imp. Firmin-Didot & Cie. Paris

MIDDLE AGES.

PAINTED AND GILDED WOODWORK OF THE XVth CENTURY. FRAGMENTS TAKEN FROM FURNITURE.

HANGING ARCHES, PANELS, BALUSTRADES, ETC.

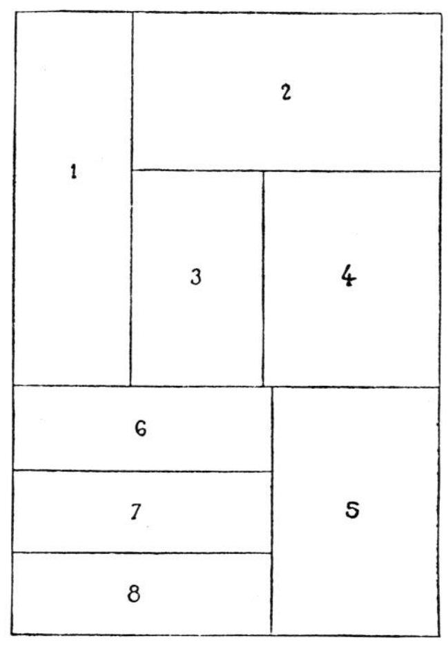

N° 1.

Panels, the inner divisions of which are those of windows of that period. In the centre an escutcheon adorned with fleurs-de-lis.

N° 2.

Double hanging arch, that is not resting upon a column. This type of decoration was used mainly in blank tracery, which is set against a full background.

N° 3.

Panel simulating a window; the main arch is divided into two parts, each a twin ogive. A fantastic animal, with the head and neck of a horse, leans on each side of the main pinion.

N° 4.

Full panel decorated with the branch of an oak bearing acorns. The leaf, of an exagerated size, is an example of the great flexibility with which the sculptors of the Flamboyant Gothic style used natural models. A sort of small dragon completes this decoration.

Nos 6, 7 and 8.

Borders which architects refer to as balustrades. Nos 6 and 8 are openwork. It was not until the second part of the Gothic epoch that it became common practice to decorate the gutters of churches with balustrades. Those of the fifteenth century are very richly decorated. N° 7, sculptured in wood, is only simulated openwork, coloured to enhance the illusion. The same applies to the ground adorned with a continuous pattern, n° 5, which is similar in line.

Brandin lith.

Imp. Firmin Didot & Cie Paris

MIDDLE AGES.

PAINTED AND GILDED WOODWORK OF THE FIFTEENTH CENTURY. FRAGMENTS OF FURNITURE. DECORATED PANELLING.

The motifs which make up this plate bear the same general characteristics as those in the plates distinguished by the symbols of the *lock* and the *whisk*. As we have already pointed out, these carved wood decorations are for the most part simple copies of the ornaments on stone constructions. Whilst making this furniture, therefore, the craftsman is still the sculptor of cathedrals and makes no allowances for the difference of the material in which he is working.

Only one example here reflects a certain freedom from architectural models: the twin arch supported by a single central column. Each arch ends in a scroll and supports a tall bracket crowned by a floral finial and decorated with animals, birds and flowered horns, instead of the usual scrolls. The high relief of this unusual sculpture stands out against a background divided into two regular parts, by the extension of the column into a light and slender finial. The artist deliberately sets off the delicacy of this blind tracery, which is borrowed from decorative ironwork, against a heavier ornamental stone style. Lastly, this rich decoration was endowed with an original sense of movement, as the two arches are slightly out of line with the tracery of the ground. Photographic documents.

Brandin lith.

Imp. Firmin Didot & Cie Paris

MIDDLE AGES.

ORNAMENTATION OF AN ARCHITECTURAL NATURE, XVth–XVIth CENTURIES.

SCULPTURES AND PAINTINGS.

THE HUMAN FIGURE IN HIERATIC DECORATIONS.

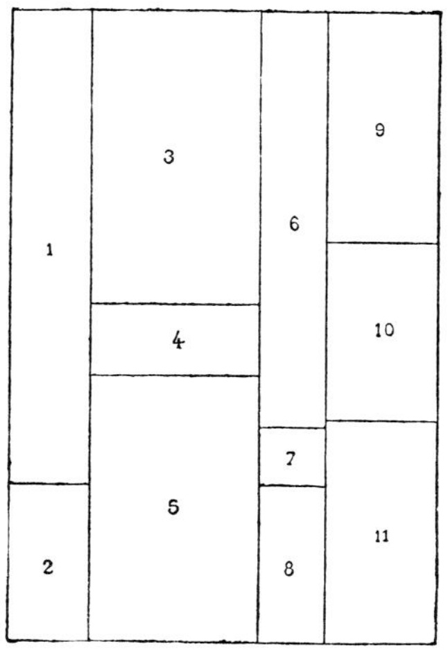

This plate is made up of three distinct elements of decoration, according to the media employed in the originals.

Nos 2, 8, 9, 10 and 11 are carved fragments of wooden furniture, which form a continuation to those illustrated on the plates bearing the symbols of the *lock*, the *whisk* and the *rosette*. They are photographic documents.

Nos 1, 4, 6 and 7 are taken from illuminations.

Nos 3 and 5 are paintings of a votive nature. The human figure is the central element but is presented in a conventional fashion which follows the models provided by stained-glass artists of the thirteenth, fourteenth and fifteenth centuries.

No 1.

This example is taken from a manuscript, no 323, of the library of the Barberini Princes, in Rome. The object on which this decoration was modelled was probably made of wood. Its construction is excellent, and the whole is in accordance with the tastes of the fifteenth century, during which many ornamentations of this type were carved.

No 6.

Border of a miniature, taken from a page attributed to Gerard von der Meire, in the breviary of cardinal Germani, library of San Marco, in Venice.

Nos 4 and 7.

These fragments representing reliefs are likewise from manuscript illuminations. They are German in nature, and the interlacing in no 4 is not only very similar to that of Albrecht Dürer, but also a direct reference to Celtic interlace.

No 5.

This painting, representing Saint Matthew and Saint James, forms part of a series showing the Apostles. Each saint is placed not in a niche, but under a canopy. Each has his name inscribed on the large halo behind his head. The ground representing a tapestry reaches the level of their eyes. This series is by Meist Wilhem, a painter in Cologne, who was master to Jan van Eyck's brother, Hubert van Eyck.

No 3.

This motif is also taken from a painting belonging to the hieratic type. The two saints stand on a stone step in front of a background which, as in the preceding example, represents a Saracen tapestry reaching up to the level of their eyes. However, the characteristic naturalism of the Dutch is here evident in the landscape above the tapestry, which is set off by an openwork of scrolls, and which felicitously replaces the gilded ground of the Byzantines.

Schmidt, lith.

Imp. Firmin-Didot & Cie. Paris

RUSSIAN.

GOLDSMITH'S WORK AND JEWELLERY IN THE XVIth CENTURY.

COPPER AND SILVER, ENAMELLED AND GEMMED.

THE IMPORTED STYLE IN THE XVIITH CENTURY.

This plate includes:

1. *Panagiae* ornaments consisting of aureoles and nimbi in the shape of tiaras and gorgets. Both are sometimes attached to one another by movable rings, as seen in n° 8. When a circular fragment projecting to one side distrupts the tiara shape of an aureole, that fragment is the nimbus of the Christ Child in the arms of his mother. The head is outlined only on the outside of painted effigies, and the aureole, though it projects out from the surface, is intended to be behind them. N°s 2, 5, 7, 8, 14, 16, 21 and 45.

2. Pendant crosses, the inner image of which determines their status as sacred jewellery. N°s 12, 18 and 24, front and back; 20, 22, 28 and 29, front and back; 30, 32 and 34, front and back; 33 and 39, front and back; 36, 37, 40, 42 and 44, front and back.

These first two series, which make up the larger part of the plate, are reproduced from life, on a scale of two-thirds the size of the originals.

3. Fragments of painted ornaments taken from Slavo-Russian manuscripts of the sixteenth century, contemporary with the jewellery shown here. The style of these fleurons is in keeping with that of the enamels. N°s 1, 3, 4, 6, 9, 10, 11, 13, 15, 17, 19, 23, 25, 27, 31, 35, 38, 41 and 43.

4. A sample of the imported style, n° 26, decorating the cover of a book dating from the end of the seventeenth century. It was the Gospel book of the Czarina Nathalie, née Naryskine, second wife to the Czar Alexis Mikhailovitch, mother of Peter the Great and regent during the latter's minority. She died in 1693.

Beneath the transformation in style, the latter work (n° 26), which is complicated and excessively rich, demonstrates the persistence of a love for magnificence characteristic of the Slavo-Russians. This was first revealed by their ancestors, if in fact, as it appears likely today, the Scythians, those ancient goldsmiths and craftsmen of gem and gold, were indeed the first to devise this brilliant form of ornamental goldwork.

Judging by our examples, the original stream of inspiration was still alive in the sixteenth century. How, then, did it come about that this stream ran dry, apparently in a matter of moments, at a time so close to our own?

The craft of the goldsmith, which is indeed a wonder of human industry, has had a striking effect upon the human imagination throughout the centuries; and, seeing that among primitive peoples superstitious value is attributed to the possession of certain kinds of stones which are used as ornaments and become amulets, it is natural that when goldsmith's work and jewellery were used to the same end, this sort of belief did not diminish. They flattered man in his instincts and the attachment they inspired must have grown still stronger, when, with time, jewels became the insignia of kinship or of a shared belief.

This is precisely what occurred among the Slavo-Russians, whose traditional tendency toward superstition is well known. In these countries, the goldsmith, with his wondrous productions, had the status of a wizard. A jewel was deemed all the more precious for being the result of a magic spell and often became the object of a superstitious attachment. In pagan times, in all the northern countries, wizardry and magic were part of religious workship. Later, they were incorporated into Christianity and the goldsmith's work of the sixteenth century Slavo-Russians, which is decorated according to ancient principles, owes to this very fusion the preservation of its national character. The special art which interests us here was the object of a long-lasting affection among the old Muscovites, who were zealous patriots and Christians, an affection sometimes approaching fanaticism.

Not until the latter part of the fifteenth century did Muscovy take its place in the political realm of Europe. Its official Christianity dates only from the dawn of the eleventh century. As naturally prone to superstition as the Slavo-Russians may be, their attachment to gold articles should come as no surprise. Indeed, eroneous beliefs about goldsmiths were quite common in Europe for a long time and it was a trading stratagem on the part of jewellery workers to appear involved in the occult sciences. The prestige of the supernatural lent to their products a mystery favorable to the price of the merchandise.

How, we must ask, can an art form with deep national roots nonetheless disappear? Fire is among the principal causes of the destruction of antique jewellery, and fire was indeed the scourge of old Muscovy. Once a fire had started in one of its wooden towns, nothing could stop it. Sooner or later, every city was inevitably devoured. Taking Moscow alone as an example, in the course of the sixteenth century, three large blazes destroyed everything there. Because they were final, the losses suffered in these catastrophes were even greater. In principle, it was not left to national art to replace what had disappeared. In fact, toward the middle of the century, following the first two big fires, Ivan IV, the Terrible or the Cruel, taking advantage of the circumstance "to enable his subjects to share in the benefits of European civilization", and having obtained permission from Charles V, commissioned the Saxon Schlit to hire foreigners to work in the service of Russia. These included scientists, artists, and craftsmen, whose numbers were to continue growing throughout subsequent reigns, and who would eventually monopolize the management of all forms of industry. The task of these immigrants was not to revive but rather to transform the former patterns of local art, and this generally took the form of a new emphasis on German styles. The introduction of foreigners caused great dissent among nationals, and partisans of the traditional continued to protest vigorously into the eighteenth century. Sacred jewels became the last refuge of traditional methods.

In ancient times, a few months would never have sufficed to train the craftsman in jewellery work. As for the goldsmith, the mere thought of his arsenal of tools — all of which, as tradition has it, he had to make himself — and of all the metals he was capable of handling, sends the mind reeling. Chemist, metallurgist, painter, calligrapher and glassmaker, the goldsmith had to be all of these in one.

From the start, the combined craft of the goldsmith-jeweller differed greatly from other forms of goldsmith's work and used special manufacturing techniques. In this kind of work, great importance was attached to the lightness of the pieces, whereas golden articles were normally prized for their weight. For this reason, among the techniques most often employed in the manufacturing of jewellery, necklaces, rings, ear-rings, headwear, and so on, embossing and punching are used alongside the braiding, knotting or twisting of metal threads and openworked ornamental foliage.

Fragility is a considerable drawback of golden jewellery, especially when there is openwork. Although silver is stronger, copper is still better. The Slavo-Russians, who were skilled in working with gold and used it for heavier finery, therefore preferred, with good reason, to use copper for their jewels. This was indeed as much the choice of artists as that of experienced craftsmen. If we turn to the classification of metals according to their density, we find that in terms of weight copper comes after platinum, gold, mercury, lead, and silver. It is in fact lighter than all of these. If gold is the most ductile of metals under the hammer or the rolling mill, tenacity — in other words the ability of a metal to support weight without breaking when it is reduced to fine threads — is found at a high level only in steel, copper and silver. Accordingly, copper also being easily fusible, its lightness coupled with its exceptional tenacity enables the craftsman to achieve extremely fine divisions without jeopardizing solidity, and thus to create very delicate workmanship.

To illustrate this we need only examine both faces of two particular pendant crosses on our plate (n°s 18 and 24, 28 and 29). If threads of gold instead of copper had been soldered to the base as settings for the enamels, these settings would have needed to be thicker and would not have had the same degree of delicacy; the pieces would have lost their subtlety and lightness. We should remember that this copper was gilded, and therefore that gold does in fact constitute the basic harmony of this colourful jewellery.

We will close this study with an examination of ornaments taken from *panagiae*. Nothing in the detail of these decorations indicates their religious function and it is thus possible to view these works as examples of styles not limited to religious art. The common principle in the ornamentation of *panagiae* is well known. In these sacred pictures, flat painted effigies are combined with the gold relief. They are oriental in origin, and it was a custom among the Byzantines to decorate images of the Virgin alone, or of the Blessed Mother with her divine child in her arms in such a fashion. A number of these painted figures were sent to Russia, which adopted the Greek style, by the monks of Mount Athos who claimed to possess the authentic portrait of the Virgin painted by Saint Luke, the Evangelist. This painting was claimed to be the model for all others. In these pictures, the holy images are haloed by an astral nimbus, either full or divided into rays of varying length. This nimbus is either gilded onto the background, or worked as a separate gold article to be attached afterwards. The *panagia*, so beloved by the Russians, owes its features to a school of the utmost austerity. In her unquestionable nobility, the Virgin appears to inhabit spheres unknown to common man. Nothing about her expresses the slightest weakness or emotion.

The solar nimbus of the ancient Madonna, whose function is to place divine beings in an imaginary world, did not appeal to the Slav. This is why, while respecting the hallowed shape of the regular nimbus, and by ingeniously using the interior outline formed by the painted figure, the jeweller found a way to make the nimbus into a piece of jewellery. Here, the rational principle of the radiating aureole has gone and a sort of tiara has been obtained. In the place of an abstract halo, this effective coronation both consecrates the sovereignty of the Virgin and humanizes her.

The palette of these decorative pieces is largely dominated by blue and green, along with the yellow of the gold.

These colours are reminiscent of Spring in the steppes, as is the vegetation used in the ornamental foliage, for the most part inspired by the weeds and wild flowers of field flora. Because of the scale of these decorations and because enamels set in relief require fullness and simplicity of form, small and simple plants were the best possible choice. They are represented in rudimentary form, with long, supple stems and large leaves with few denticles.

What is most manifest about this jewellery is its Asian character. Byzantine influence is visible only at the centre of the pendant crosses in the form of the Christian insignia, which were consecrated by the Orthodox Church.

Imported styles and art forms do not of their own leave roots as tenacious as those we have seen. The art of the Slavo-Russians, which, particularly through jewellery, fuelled a popular mythology which found itself mixed with the official doctrines, was a complex and charming expression of the truly poetic imagination of a whole race.

Panagiae Ornaments

N° 2.

Nimbus of both the Virgin and Jesus. Gilded and enamelled copper with a few coloured stones. One specific insignia is present in the child's nimbus, the gorget, designating the leader. Gorgets which appear to have belonged primarily to northern Asians were found in the treasure of Petrossa, which is thought to have been the property of a Hunnish king of the third century. Their shape is more or less that of a crescent. It may be that the design of several of the gorgets in our *panagiae* and in the inner crosses of several of the pendant jewels had a dual purpose. On the one hand, they are the emblem of the leader or chief, while on the other they may also represent the Greek letter omega and its meaning, the end of all things. The ground of the piece is stippled.

N° 5.

Nimbus of the Christ Child, surrounding a bonnet-shaped crown. This piece was accompanied by a royal gorget. Gilded and enamelled copper.

N° 7.

Nimbus of both the Virgin and Jesus. Gilded, enamelled and openwork copper.

N° 8.

Nimbus of the Christ Child with gorget. Gilded and enamelled copper decorated with pearls.

N° 14.

Nimbus of the Christ Child. Gilded and enamelled copper.

N° 16.

Gorget. Gilded and enamelled copper, with a central stone.

N° 21.

Nimbus. Gilded and enamelled copper, solid metal, stippled ground.

N° 45.

Nimbus of the Christ Child. Gilded, enamelled and openwork copper.

Pendant Crosses

N° 12.

Small cross of engraved gold. It is finely openworked and is not enamelled.

N°s 18 and 24.

Front and back of a jewel whose sacred character is indicated by the small cross in the centre front. This cross is designed according to the Oriental rite. The common usage in the Orient, where the Greek language retained its pre-eminence, of the equi-branched Greek cross appears to be a reminder of the letter X, the first letter of the Greek Christogram, formed by four right-angles. However, the Greek cross was a symbol older than Christianity. In order to avoid confusion, the Greeks chose to include the name of Jesus in their depictions of the cross by adding a small diagonal bar to the upright of the cross, a clearer reminder of the Greek X than the equi-branched cross on its own.

This pendant cross is made of gilded and enamelled copper, decorated with small stones and turquoises. It is the gem of this collection.

N° 20.

Small Greek cross. Gold with five white stones set in relief and four small coloured stones in the corners.

N° 22.

Gilded and enamelled copper cross. This one has inscriptions at the ends of its arms, and, hanging from it, the gorget of the sovereign.

N°s 28 and 29.

Back and front of a pendant cross. The top part of the cross is carved *en cabochon* with a hole for the cord. A gorget in the shape of an omega also figures on the inner cross. This insignia recalls the God of the Jews who is the end of all things. Gilded and enamelled copper, adorned with semi-precious stones.

N° 30.

Small cross of gilded and enamelled copper with radiating diagonals. A gorget figures on the cross inside the jewel and there are inscriptions on its four arms.

N°s 32 and 34.

Front and back of a silver cross, enamelled on the front and engraved on the back. A gorget figures on the inner cross, as do inscriptions on the four arms of the jewel.

N°s 33 and 39.

Front and back of an enamelled silver cross. At the top is an inscription. The ends of the remaining three arms are *en cabochon*.

N° 36.

Engraved silver cross. This piece is not a sacred jewel.

N° 37.

Jade cross mounted in gilded copper and decorated with semi-precious stones and pearls. Christ is engraved on the cross.

N° 40.

Gilded and embossed copper cross, decorated with coloured stones set in relief. Engraved Christ.

N°s 42 and 44.

Back and front of a silver cross, with gilded front. This openwork jewel is adorned with coloured stones set in relief and is sacred in character.

Fragments from Illuminated Manuscripts of the XVIth Century

All the fragments are taken from breviaries and prayer books belonging to Russian libraries and collections.

N° 26.

Cover of a Gospel book belonging to the Czarina Nathalie. This metalwork from the end of the XVIIth century is very richly decorated and displays a great variety of techniques including engraving, enamelling, the setting in relief and the inlaying of semi-precious stones, and intaglio. The ornamentation is evenly distributed across the cover according to no apparent general plan. This type of binding is thus essentially different from what is known of the Byzantines and of those who imitated them in the decoration of prayer book covers. It has nothing in common with the well-known style of binding where a border frames a scene engraved in relief, in metal or ivory. The line is of lesser importance to the Slavs than harmony of colour and pattern. It is important to note, however, that this piece is made up of elements which lack the local naiveté of the earlier works. The shape of some of the areas of solid metal is borrowed from the Persians while the somewhat heavy foliated scrolls which tie the pattern together are inspired by the Greek acanthus.

RUSSIAN. RUSSE. RUSSISCHE

Spiegel lith   Imp. Firmin-Didot & Cie Paris

RUSSIAN.

THE ORNAMENTATION OF SIXTEENTH CENTURY MANUSCRIPTS.

The documents on this plate are taken from three manuscripts and illustrate the transformation wrought by the Slavs upon the Celtic interlace pattern, from which they began by eliminating the animal principle. Most noticeable is the appearance in these patterns of motifs inspired by plant life.

N°s 9 and 11 are combinations of the flat Celtic interlace pattern. However, in n° 9, small rounded knots symmetrically distributed along the interlacing lend it a somewhat plant-like aspect which is confirmed by the flowers depicted in the corners of the motif.

In n° 11, there are no plant-like knots, but the upper corner is similarly formed by a flower, while developing foliage appears in the lower corner.

The flat Celtic interlace pattern is still the principle element in n°s 2, 12, and 14, which are taken from a second manuscript. The rectilinear geometry of their design appears to indicate Arabic or Persian influence. The Slav craftsman, however, has added a new note, in the shape of the plant-like stalk on the side of each of these motifs.

The other motifs shown in this plate, which all belong to a new style resembling woven esparto in blossom, are part of a third manuscript. N° 6 is the richest example of this new, particularly felicitous style of ornamentation in which a sense of opulence is achieved through very simple means.

These motifs are taken from manuscripts in the Imperial Library of Saint Petersburg.

Lestel, lith. Imp. Firmin Didot & Cie Paris

RUSSIAN.

THE ORNAMENTATION OF SLAVO-RUSSIAN MANUSCRIPTS

OF THE XVIth CENTURY.

BLACK AND WHITE PLATE.

The present drawings are tracings of the originals by Nicolas Vassilief, an engraver from Saint Petersburg who had easy access to the museums and private collections of the city.

According to Russian scholars, native master craftsmen, free of the exotic influences of the Greeks on the one hand and the Lombard master builders on the other, could be found in Russia as early as the twelfth and thirteenth centuries. The Lombards had been called upon by Andrej Georgievitch to build the Cathedral of the Assumption of the Virgin Mary in the city of Vladimir. In the course of ensuing centuries, similar edifices were built in many places including in Moscow in the fifteenth and sixteenth centuries. The Mongol invasion impeded relations with the Greek world and the ensuing isolation appears to have contributed to the originality of Slavo-Russian ornamentation which resembles neither the Byzantine style nor its derivative, the Romanesque style.

The Celtico-Scandinavian influence is quite apparent in the documents reproduced here. The Slavo-Russian signature is, nevertheless, unmistakable in the combining of interlace and figures, and in the organization and distribution of these ornaments, so ingeniously and solidly conceived. Indeed, not one of these motifs lacks logic in its construction: every one of them could be manufactured.

Slavo-Russian manuscripts first appeared in the eleventh century and were produced until the eighteenth century. The spontaneous style of Russian ornamentation, however, is limited to the period between the twelfth and sixteenth centuries, before the adoption of Western taste in the seventeenth century.

The specific sources of the drawings in our plate are unknown but similar ornamentations are found in religious manuscripts of the fourteenth century.

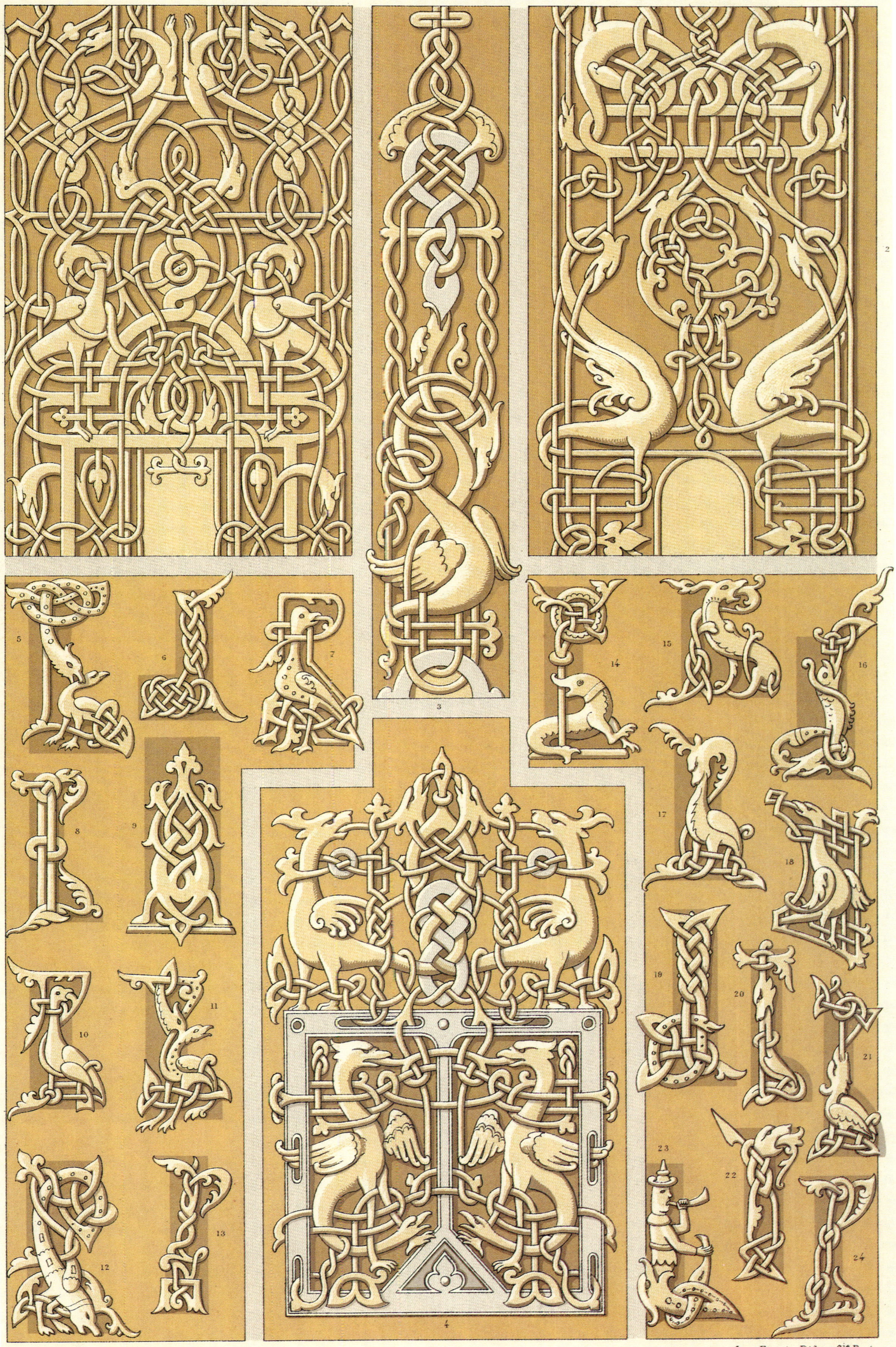

Schmidt lith. Imp. Firmin-Didot & Cie, Paris

RUSSIAN.

ORNAMENTATION FROM THE XIIth TO XVth CENTURIES:

ENGRAVINGS AND SCRIPTURAL DOCUMENTS.

BLACK AND WHITE PLATE.

(See notice accompanying the plate identified by the symbol of the *flat-iron*)

For the most part, the motifs on this plate are from the thirteenth and fourteenth centuries. Several, showing evidence of Asian influence, are from the fifteenth century, namely nos 7, 10, 13, 17, 19, 20 and 22.

For several centuries, the imitation of Western art took precedence over Russian art and its traditions. However, more characteristically Russian styles of ornamentation did appear on curiously engraved platters, ewers, samovars decorated with archaic animals, inscriptions in Slavonic letters, and so forth.

The possibilities inherent in this style are illustrated by the rosette paten designs, nos 4 and 7, with their borders, nos 8 and 9; by the rectangular surfaces, nos 11 and 12, covered by interlinking patterns; by the corners of nos 1 and 10, the florets, nos 2, 13, 17, 18, 20 and 21, the initials, nos 15, 16, and fragments nos 3, 5, 6, 14, 19 and 22.

Schmidt lith.

Imp. Firmin-Didot & Cie, Paris

RUSSIAN.

ENGRAVINGS AND ILLUMINATIONS.

PANELS, BORDERS, HINGES, ORNAMENTAL KNOTS, FLORETS.

These motifs no longer strictly represent the original local Slavo-Russian style. They do, however, demonstrate the ingenuity, clarity and rhythm which are typical of the earlier style. In general, they are well conceived and nicely composed. Some of the patterns are a late development of the Celtic interlace design, either enriched by Byzantine exfoliations, or enlivened by the interplay of the fine threads of an arabesque. Most of these coils have the attributes of ironworks. Indeed, the elements of this ornamentation are, by nature, quite simple and it is the diverse combinations of these elements which give an impression of abundance. Everything here is imaginary: the imitation of nature plays no part in this style.

The source of these motifs is given in the caption to the plate distinguished by the symbol of the *flat-iron*.

Schmidt, lith. Imp. Firmin-Didot & Cie, Paris

RUSSIAN.

GOLD ARTICLES, ENGRAVED AND CARVED ORNAMENTATION OF ROSETTES AND BORDERS OF PLATES.

These documents complement those plates identified by the symbols of the *flat-iron*, the *hat* and the *rat*. Their source is given in the notice accompanying the first of these plates.

Despite apparent exotic influences, these ornaments, which vary in period and style, retain the essentially rhythmic quality characteristic of the Slavo-Russian style. The construction is always logical and legible, no matter how complicated the pattern may be.

RUSSE.

RUSSIAN. RUSSISCH

Schmidt lith. Imp. Firmin Didot & Cie, Paris

RUSSIAN.

ENGRAVINGS.

ORNAMENTAL KNOTS, CORNERS, BORDERS AND GROUND MOTIFS.

These documents are part of the series of plates bearing the symbols of the *flat-iron*, the *hat*, the *bayonet* and the *rat*, the source of which is indicated in the caption to the first of these plates.

As previously remarked, despite the deviations in local style due to outside influences, a common principle remains in all our samples. The interweaving of these surface ornamentations always appears logical, forming the links that would be necessary to create a real openwork construction. The painstaking care shown by the designer–craftsman lends a unity to these various works which is all the more remarkable when we remember that, because of their geographical location, the Russians were exposed to two important artistic currents. Yet, regardless of how much they may have borrowed from the Asian arts, the ornamentation of their metalwork is not derived from that of Persian ceramics, or the isolated motifs repeated on Hindu surfaces, nor does it owe anything to the whimsical ornamental foliage of Chinese and Japanese *cloisonnés*, or to the smaller motifs found on lacquerwork and porcelain.

Schmidt lith.

Imp. Firmin-Didot & Cie Paris

RUSSIAN.

ENGRAVINGS — CORNERS OF BORDERS.

This page completes the series of ornamentations from various periods which served to decorate Slavo-Russian metal work. The source of these motifs is mentioned in the caption accompanying the plate distinguished by the symbol of the *flat-iron*. This style is further displayed in the subsequent plates bearing the symbols of the *hat*, the *bayonet*, the *rat*, and the *crane*. The colouring typical of these ornaments is illustrated in the plates bearing the symbols of the *brush* and the *drum*, as in the plate representing Armenian motifs, identified by the symbol of the *scythe*, which, although they have a different kind of splendour, are nevertheless related to those we have seen.

These corner motifs will be of great assistance to those seeking to apply this decorative style. By no means primitive in style, these ornaments take partly after Asian art, partly after the European productions of the second half of the sixteenth century and the first half of the seventeenth. However, as previously mentioned, the survival of a local character is detectable in the logical development of the interweaving.

The design of these engravings, which has the range of sculpture, as exemplified by the above fragments, further supports our opinion that despite its symmetrical regularity, Slavo-Russian ornamentation is never dull.

Spiégel, lith. Imp. Firmin Didot & Cie, Paris

ARMENIAN.

ORNAMENTATION OF MANUSCRIPTS.

These motifs were taken from a prayer book of uncertain origin. They are undoubtedly Armenian in style, and may have been executed in the sixteenth century, though most probably somewhat earlier. Indeed, the style of ornamentation shows evidence of very ancient sources. This is clearly demonstrated if one compares these designs with the illuminations taken from a Greek manuscript painted in Asia Minor around 800, three of which are reproduced in the Greco-Byzantine plate identified by the symbol of the *saucepan*. These motifs (n°s 2, 3 and 4) are specimens of Greek ornamentation modified by Asian influences. The present examples, from a later period, indicate the growing Asian influence on Armenian ornamentation. It is remarkable, however, that despite the Indo-Persian influence so noticeable in most of the floret motifs, the Armenians were able to retain a style of their own. This may be partly due to the effect of other influences, such as that of the Slavo-Russians, whose emphasis on logical interweaving is likewise encountered in several of the present designs.

ARMÉNIEN

ARMENIAN

ARMENIER

Lestel lith.

Imp. Firmin Didot & Cie Paris

MIDDLE AGES.

MARGINAL ORNAMENTATION INSPIRED BY ENAMELLED GOLDSMITH'S WORK AND JEWELLERY.

PAINTING ON MANUSCRIPTS — XVTH CENTURY.

These manuscript illustrations, which borrow so openly from the art of XVth century Italian and, in some cases, Flemish jewellery, underscore the specifically European tendency to use relief for emphasis in the ornamentation of goldsmith's work and jewellery. This is quite different from Islamic decorative styles in Persia and India where colour is given precedence in compositions, and the use of enamel is limited to simple forms and outlines on level surfaces, as exemplified in our plates by Koranic inscriptions (plates distinguished by the symbols of the *thermometer* and the *jack*), by Persian and Indian daggers (plate identified by the symbol of the *arm*), and by Tibetan copperwork (plate identified by the symbol of the *playing cards*).

On the other hand, European ornamental surfaces became progressively more intricate. In the Middle Ages, and for as long as the art of enamelled metalworking and jewellery was modelled on Byzantine prototypes, complicated relief decoration remained relatively rare. As a result of the Scythian movement, however, and with the setting in relief of coloured stones, relief engravings of varying depths, and the application of filigree — all of which were widely practised —, the features of goldsmith's work and jewellery were transformed into something very different from the plaque enamels of Egypt and ancient Greece. Gradually, engraved scrolls of delicately foliated ornament replaced filigree work until finally relief engraving became the dominant ornamental mode, with or without enamels, set with coloured stones and adorned with pearls. Furthermore, in addition to opaque and translucent enamelling, ornamentalists introduced painting on primed surfaces, in the manner of Limoges enamels, thus fashioning the ornamental scroll structure into a mount for small paintings inserted in the jewellery.

In the present illustrations, the ornamentation is imitative of bas-reliefs on a metallic ground and of foliated scrolls in openworked metal, carved in full relief and set against a velvet foil.

N° 1.

Roman missal of the fifteenth century; Brera Library, Milan.

N° 11.

Gradual from Siena. Page painted by Girolamo da Cremona.

N°s 2, 7, and 10.

Fragments from large and small margins, and initial N from a page of the Bible of Mathias Corvin; Vatican Library, Rome.

N° 3.

Codex n° 323, from the Barberini Library in Rome.

N°s 4, 5, 6 and 9.

Choir books from the Cathedral of Florence, sixteenth century. Antiphonary. Fragments from a page painted by Fra Eustachio.

N° 8.

Breviary of Cardinal Grimani. San Marco Library, in Venice. Page painted by Hans Memling.

RENAISSANCE.

ENAMELLED JEWELLERY. — XVth–XVIth CENTURIES.

This and the following plate distinguished by the symbol of the *bed*, display a selection of illustrations taken from Italian and Flemish manuscripts. They provide a historical overview which is all the more valuable considering that so little of the jewellery of this period survives.

In the second half of the fifteenth century and the first half of the sixteenth, marginal illustrations were the work of miniaturists trained in the goldsmiths' shops of Italy, in accordance with a tradition common to architects, sculptors, and painters. These illuminations are therefore imprinted with the very principles of the precise art of the goldsmith and, beneath their flourishes, the structure of these ornaments most often appears to follow a discernible logic. In fact, many marginal ornaments were reproductions of actual pieces of jewellery.

This practice of reproducing real jewels first came to our attention upon an examination of the famed choir books of the Cathedral of Siena, and in particular of those pages painted by Liberale di Giacomo da Verona, who came to Siena in 1466, where he illuminated five antiphonaries over a period of nine years. This miniaturist, who is a true master in the composition of scenes which he inserted in the initials of these very large choir books — initials which measured between fifteen and twenty centimetres in height — was trained by the masters of Padua and Verona, including the famous Mantegna, renowned for his interpretations of classical subjects. Into the margins of the Siena choir books, Liberale introduced entire pieces of jewellery, which are not blended in with the rest of the ornamentation but which stand on their own as they might have been displayed in the jeweller's shop. Other miniaturists soon followed in the steps of Liberale, among them artists such as Giovanni di Giulano Boccardi da Firenze, known as "il Boccardino Vecchio", the Dominican Fra Eustachio, Attavante, Litti di Filippo Corbizi, the mosaicist and miniaturist Monte di Giovanni, Antonio di Girolamo, and others.

Choir books from the Cathedral of Siena, Gradual and Antiphonaries. — Nos 1, 2, 3, 10, 11, 12, 16, 18, 19, and 21.

Choir books from the Cathedral of Florence. — Nos 7 and 22.

Fifteenth-century Roman missal from the Brera Museum in Milan. — Nos 5 and 6.

Small missal from the end of the fifteenth century, Barberini Library, in Rome. — Nos 4, 14, 17 and 20.

Breviary of Cardinal Grimani, San Marco Library in Venice. — Nos 8, 9, 13 and 15. Concerning this jewellery, which is Flemish, see the caption accompanying the plate identified by the symbol of the *bed*.

Spiégel, lith. Imp. Firmin-Didot & Cie, Paris

RENAISSANCE.

ENAMELLED JEWELLERY. — XIVth–XVIth CENTURIES.

Under the influence and discipline of the masters of Pisa, Padua and Verona and of the Florentine colony, the great movement of the Renaissance was marked primarily by a return to classical Antiquity. Nevertheless, a tendency toward naturalism was also manifest, at times imitative of the Gothic art which influenced Giotto himself. Partisans of this style persisted for a long time among the Sienese and in some cases also among Florentine artists. The Flemish contingent may have played a part in the survival of this taste for it is certain that commercial exchange between the Flemish and Italian goldworking trades, which was very active in the fifteenth century, allowed each to influence the other.

In our plate, nº 2, translucent enamel on relief, appears to be a bodice ornament. Nº 21, a belt cord, is also meant to be worn as an ornament in place of the rosary. Besides the many brooches, pendants, and pin heads, there are also pieces, such as nº 67, which were worn around the neck and used as a portable oratory at prayer time. Nº 7, with its paschal lamb, is a small devotional object, decorated in a fashion similar to the technique of Limoges enamels. The remarkable little piece, nº 27, attributed to Liberale di Giacomo, is a decorated initial, an M with three downstrokes in the Gothic style, in which the middle stroke has been foreshortened to allow the depiction of the scene of the visitation of Saint Elizabeth by the Virgin Mary. It was a common practice to truncate a letter in this way to accommodate the picture. This *pax* is painted with enamel, and the reliefs of the ornamentation itself are enamelled and adorned with stones and pearls. The dimension of the original painting conforms to the usual format of the *pax* which is 17 centimetres in height.

Choir books from the Cathedral of Siena, Gradual and Antiphonaries. — Nºs 1, 2, 3, 5, 6, 9, 10, 11, 12, 17, 18, 19, 20, 23, 26, 28, 31, 33, 34, 35, 36, 37, 41, 43, 44, 48, 49, 50, 51, 53, 54, 55, 56, 58, 59, 62, 63, 65, 68 and 69.

Choir books from the Cathedral of Florence. — Nºs 7, 15, 22, 24 and 27.

Small missal from the end of the fifteenth century, Barberini Library, Rome. — Nºs 16, 60 and 66.

Urbino Library, Rome. — Nºs 21, 45 and 46.

Breviary of Mathias Corvin, Rome. — Nºs 61 and 64.

Missal of Sant'Ambrogio, Milan. — Nº 38.

Breviary of Cardinal Grimani, San Marco Library, Venice. — Nºs 4, 8, 13, 14, 25, 29, 30, 32, 34, 39, 40, 42, 52 and 67.

Spiégel, lith. Imp. Firmin Didot & Cie Paris

RENAISSANCE.

ORNAMENTATION OF MANUSCRIPTS, XVth CENTURY.

FLORENTINE SCHOOL.

These fragments are the uprights of frames taken from the pages of a manuscript in the San Marco Library in Venice. The book, by Marziano Capella, deals with the *Marriage of Mercury and Philology* and the *Seven Liberal Arts*. The illuminations are by the famed Florentine miniaturist, Attavante.

In the fifteenth century, Italian miniaturists were clearly separate from painters and specialization was already the rule. Among these specialists, Attavante attracted attention by turning this marginal style into great art, treated in miniature.

At a time and in a country where Greek and Roman writings were being transcribed in prodigious quantity, and the authors of the day were turning to these sources, miniaturists were faced with the necessity of abandoning the medieval formulae for illumination, the indigenous flora and the whimsical leafy ornaments of the last part of the Ogival period. As with the other arts, Florence led the way in reforming miniature painting, and the miniaturists of Cosimo de Medici and his son Piero were the first to find inspiration in the art of Antiquity and to introduce into their regular and orderly borders elements such as jewels, coins, cameos, intaglios, and mythological nudes.

In manuscripts like that of Marziano Capella, in which the gods of Mount Olympus are dressed in Florentine clothes, the anachronistic costumes are yet another source of decorative splendour, as may be seen in the fifth of the vertical panels in our plate, in which the beautiful scrolls painted in black and white against a golden ground are set off by the figures painted in full colour in the medallions. The top figure of the centre upright in this plate is a Mercury, and exemplifies how mythological characters were then treated.

Attavante, inspired by Greek and Roman sculptors whose masterpieces he had access to in the Medici collection, appears to have striven primarily for purity of line rather than brilliance of composition. His grace and passion, absolutely Attic in spirit, are closer to Greek than to Roman art.

The composition of manuscript borders, which attained in the hands of miniaturist masters a truly new level of sharpness and distinction, was one of the most powerful means of conveying the ideas of the Renaissance. Books, which are easy to carry, went a long way in spreading their teachings and miniaturists such as Attavante, the regular supplier of the brilliant king of Hungary, Mathias Corvin, were internationally acclaimed and greatly in demand.

Charpentier lith. Imp. Firmin-Didot & Cie Paris

RENAISSANCE.

ORNAMENTATION OF MANUSCRIPTS. — XVth CENTURY.

FLORENTINE SCHOOL.

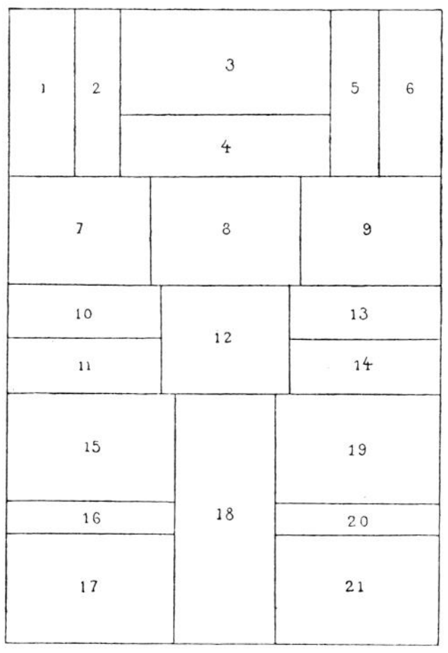

1. Vertical panel n° 1, with an alternately red and blue ground beneath golden scrolls goes together with n° 19 of the present plate, which has a blue ground with golden scrolls, and with initial n° 8, the ground of which is green and damasked.

2. Vertical panel n° 2, with golden scrolls on a blue and gold ground is on the same page as n° 11, which has a gold ground and ornamental foliage in black and white.

3. Vertical panel n° 3, with a blue and gold ground, and blue scrolls goes together with n° 4, which has green scrolls on a red ground, and with the fragment of the vertical panel n° 1, with foliage in black and white on a green ground.

4. Vertical panel n° 4 with its blue and red ground and golden scrolls is on the same page as n° 21, which also has golden scrollwork but on a blue ground only, and with initial n° 7, which has a red ground beneath golden foliated scrolls.

5. Finally, vertical panel n° 5, which has foliated scrolls in black and white against a gold ground, as does its small side n° 6, is from the same ornamental frame as n° 3, with black and white scrollwork on a blue ground.

Vertical panel fragment n° 18, with a blue ground and black and white foliage is from the same border as n° 17, which has a green background and golden scrollwork, as is the initial n° 9 with its gold background and foliated black and white scrolls.

The small running borders shown as n°s 2, 5, 16 and 20 are repeating motifs used to fill in areas where there is no relief, similar to the ground of the initial n° 8.

Charpentier, lith. Imp. Firmin Didot & Cie Paris

RENAISSANCE.

PAINTED ORNAMENTATION IN THE FIRST PART OF THE XVIth CENTURY IN ITALY.

THE FLORENTINE SCHOOL, MONOCHROME DECORATION.

In this plate, motifs n°s 1, 14 and 15, which are reproduced in their entirety, and n°s 4, 7, and 10, which come from parts of an initial, are from the Florentine school, represented by one of its most illustrious masters, Monte di Giovanni, who flourished between 1500 and 1528. He was a powerful artist who brought to the art of miniature painting the advantages of an education received in the goldsmith's shop, coupled with a proficiency in the art of mosaic. It is assuredly this latter quality which lends remarkable range to his works.

The style of ornamentation practised by Monte di Giovanni di Favilla allies grace with strength and reveals knowledge of the acanthus of Antiquity which is manipulated with the freedom and imagination of a true goldsmith, who has no need to resort to the voluble flourishes of the scribe.

There is evidence, in these works, of the vigorous training of the mosaicist, who, knowing the means at his disposal are limited, is aware that to achieve variety in colour ornamentation, he must not exploit all the possibilities of colour in every scene, or every piece, but that, on the contrary, he must choose for each of them a dominant, accentuated tone, in such a way as to obtain true variety through parallels which are the basis of a superior decorative richness.

N° 14 is also an initial, an M with three downstrokes, all of which the artist has retained since the middle stroke was not an obstacle in the overall composition of the scene. This beautiful letter of architectonic design is also treated in a powerful monochrome, the unity of which forms a felicitous contrast with the subject painted in full colour. The scene depicts the temptation of Jesus by the Devil. These miniatures by Monte de Giovanni are found in choir books from the Cathedral of Florence.

Fragments n°s 2, 6, 8, and 9 are taken from the Gradual of the Cathedral of Siena, and date from the period of Liberale di Giacomo.

N°s 13 and 16, the character of which is more modern, are found in the Antiphonaries of the Cathedral of Florence and are taken from the pages painted by Antonio di Girolamo.

Fragments n°s 3, 11, 12 and 17 are taken from the choir books of the Charterhouse of Pavia, Brera Library, Milan.

N° 5 is from the Missal of Clement VII, Chigi Palace Library, Rome.

Bénard lith.

Imp. Firmin Didot & Cie Paris

RENAISSANCE.

XVth–XVIth CENTURIES, MARGINAL DECORATIONS OF MANUSCRIPTS.

SCATTERED FLOWER MOTIFS, SYMBOLIC ORNAMENTATION.

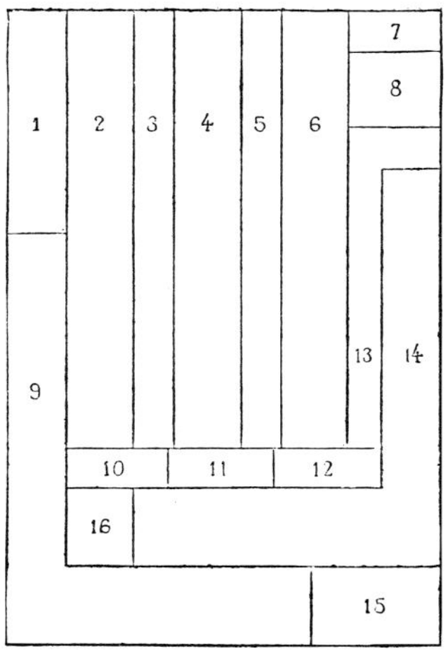

The architectural ornamentation of monuments in the florid or flamboyant Gothic style, which was inspired by plant-life and sought to imitate natural effects, led manuscript illuminators of the second half of the sixteenth century and first half of the seventeenth to resort to similar decorative sources. Indeed, floral decorations appeared in the margins of manuscripts in the form of fruits and flowers on fine stems seemingly scattered around the border of the page, thus creating a sort of frame for a painted scene or, more often, for a text enlivened by *vignettes*.

Nos 1, 7, 8, 9, 11, 13, 14 and 15

Fragments showing how the artist solved the problem of filling large or small margins of manuscript pages and also of the way in which colour was used. Nos 1 and 15. Birds and flowers painted according to nature alternating with kale leaf whorls painted in bronze tones. Nos 9 and 14. Wide margins laden with flowers in full bloom. Nos 7 and 13. Narrow margins decorated with a succession of flower buds. No 11. Elongated stem of a strawberry plant with its fruit. No 8. Curly kale leaf initial, painted in monochrome, and decorated with a naturally coloured flower.

No 12.

Christogram. These motifs are from the Roman Breviary, also known as the Breviary of Cardinal Grimani. This famous and important manuscript is the work of Flemish artists, including Hans Memling, Gerald of Antwerp and Lieven of Ghent. It was created after 1471.

Nos 2, 3, 4, 5, 6, 10 and 12

Wide and narrow margins from the *Prayers to the Virgin Mary* manuscript made for Alessandro de' Medici, first duke of Florence, born in 1510 and assassinated in 1537, a few months after his marriage to Margaret, the illegitimate daughter of Charles V of Spain. Their portraits face each other in our plate.

In addition to scattered flowers, animals, and insects, the Florentine ornamentalist has included elements of a very different kind, placed at regular intervals. Cameos, treated according to the classical style, hark back to distant ancestors; the splendour of gems is added to that of the floral universe; golden symmetrical scrolls (see no 4) form a sharp contrast with the capricious swirls of the curly kale. The choice of these elements often has a symbolic meaning. The pearls, for example stand for the name *Margarita*, which means pearl.

No 10, which is taken from the top of the same page, is decorated with an inset garnet, accompanied on each side by a green branch tied with a ribbon on which is written the word *semper* (always). The branches are joined together by the stem of a strawberry plant bearing fruit. This manuscript, codex 1232, is part of the collection of the Corsini Library in Rome.

Mathieu lith.

Imp. Firmin Didot & Cie. Paris

RENAISSANCE.

THE DECORATION OF RUGS FOLLOWING ORIENTAL TYPES.

ITALY. — XVth CENTURY.

These examples are reproduced from paintings in the Fine Art Academy of Florence and the Academy of Ferrare. The first one, with a black ground, is a wall-hanging from a Ghirlandaio painting and the second is a table-cloth from a painting by Carpaccio. Both designs are clearly inspired by the Oriental tradition.

The ornamental pattern of the wall-hanging is woven in the woof of the fabric and is reminiscent of a marquetry design. The geometrical distribution of the repeated motifs, which are both varied in design and delicate, lends to this work an air of tranquility and opulence. The white so skilfully used in this composition, whether in uninterrupted lines, small splashes, or in broader shapes, is the key to its brilliance.

The embroidered velvet table-cloth is very different in character. Its design is in the arabesque style. The border, which in fact forms the main ornament, is made up of a series of similar motifs, varied only by the inversion of the patterns. This design is more Persian in character than anything else, for at the hands of the Persians the arabesque often takes on a plant-like aspect. The same is true of the central motif, although there is a Byzantine touch to the design of its centre. The subtle and refined colouring of these arabesques is most felicitous and is distributed in such a way as to preserve the rich imposing unity of the velvet ground.

Debenais, lith.

Imp. Firmin-Didot & Cie. Paris

RENAISSANCE.

FRAMES IN THE ARCHITECTONIC STYLE.

ENAMELLED GOLD.

PAINTING ON MANUSCRIPTS. XVTH, XVITH CENTURIES.

The taste for architectural constructions manifested by the master painters of Italy in the fifteenth century, which was in keeping with the great movement of the Renaissance towards the principles of Antiquity, was soon adopted by manuscript decorators. The architectonic style, which was added to the foliated ornaments already in the margins, introduced great variety to the framing of miniatures. This style grew in importance in the last part of the fifteenth century and enjoyed great favour in France throughout the sixteenth century. For the most part, the designs of marginal decorations in the architectonic genre are borrowed from the goldsmiths' work of the period.

In this plate, we have included, in their vertical entirety, examples of borders in the architectonic style, as well as fragments of motifs which one can easily reconstitute following the principle of those which are complete. Furthermore, in order to illustrate the relation between the products of the goldsmith and the architectonic constructions of great painting, an intermediary example is shown here, which, though it is not goldsmith's work in the strict sense, nevertheless partakes of all the industries of the period relating to vividly coloured and decorated constructions. In the original, the examples n°s 1 and 2 make up an entire scene, the two sides of which are reproduced here to give a sense of its architectonic composition. This is intended to appear as a building with an inside room, with a linear perspective deep enough for the scene to extend back to the horizon. According to the inscription on the base, the subject is the Passover celebrated by Josiah. The golden Ark of the Covenant is set on a marble altar where a fire is burning, and the Jews are kneeling on either side.

Motif n° 10 is taken from a manuscript of Dante's *Divine Comedy*, Ms. n° 365 in the library of the Vatican. This magnificent book belonged to Frederico, first duke of Urbino, and was transcribed in 1482. Its miniature paintings are in the style of the Umbrian school. The medallion inserted in this arch is from the same volume and possibly also depicts enamels painted on glass laid on a ground.

N°s 4, 5, 6, 8, 9 and 13 are found in manuscript n° 1015, from the Corsini Library in Rome. The small fragments, n°s 3 and 12, are taken from a twelfth-century Book of Hours in the Bibliothèque nationale (Ms. n° 296). The architectonics of these borders is similar to that of n°s 7 and 14 which may thus serve to complete the set. The manuscript from which the latter samples are taken, also in the Bibliothèque nationale (Ms. n° 304), is a sixteenth-century *Praeces piae* containing 40 beautiful miniatures, 21 of which have an architectural border. This is typical of many Books of Hours from this period, most of which are French works.

Bénard lith.

Imp. Firmin-Didot & Cie Paris

RENAISSANCE.

ORNAMENTAL ARCHITECTONIC CONSTRUCTIONS.

THE HUMAN FIGURE IN A CONVENTIONAL SETTING.

PAINTINGS AND MINIATURES, XVTH–XVITH CENTURIES.

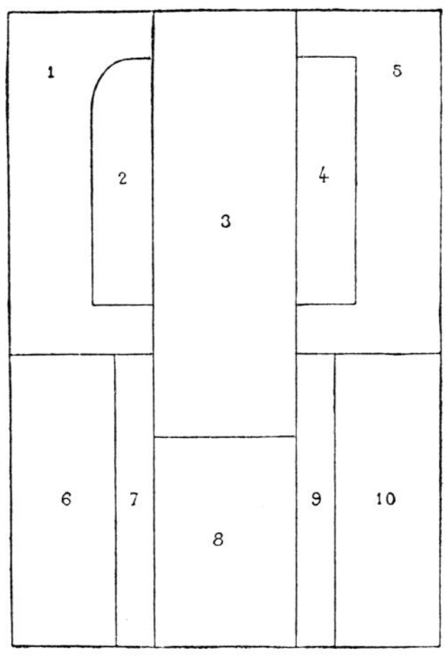

Nº 1.

Fragment of a page of the manuscript of Dante's *Divine Comedy* created for one of the dukes of Urbino (Library of the Vatican).

This rich composition is by Giulio Clovio or Giulio Grovata, known as Clovio, who was the student first of Girolamo dai Libri, then of Jules Romain. Born in 1498, he died in 1578.

Nº 2.

Fragment of a page border from a fifteenth-century manuscript of the Minerva Library in Rome.

The principle of this construction is that of a series of niches, each containing an angel playing a period instrument. The series is interrupted by the coats of arms of Peter II, duke of Bourbon, and of Anne of France, daughter of Louis XI, who married in 1474.

Nº3.

Saint Helena, mother of Constantine, holding the wood of the real cross which, according to legend, she discovered in the ruins of a pagan temple. This painting is by J.V. Melem.

Nº4.

Fragment of the border of a miniature in manuscript nº 1015 from the Corsini Library in Rome.

This document dates from the sixteenth century and its fanciful architecture is in the Italian style. The flexibility of this genre afforded many possibilities to the artist, as illustrated by the two neighbouring examples in our plate. Nº 4 frames a vertical scene in two sections: the *Spiritual Life*, depicted in the Heavens, and the *Profane Life* shown in the lower part of the painting.

Nº 5.

Page border framing a miniature which represents a single scene in heightened perspective. This fragment is taken from the same manuscript as nº 4. The subject of the scene is Saint Denis wearing a bishop's vestment and holding the pastoral crosier in one hand, and his mitred head in the other. He is accompanied by Saint Rustic and Saint Eleuther.

Nºs 7 and 9 are taken from the same source and are in a similar style.

Nº 6.

Votive painting: vertical panel painted by Israel von Meckenem. The perspective of the recess is deeper than that of the niche. The joining of the arches at the top of the painting, however, lends to the structure the aspect of a classical niche.

Nº 8.

Votive painting, the principal subject of which stands out against an architectural frame which serves as an intermediary between the figure of the saint and a charming open air landscape. This is a type of composition often used during this period, when an effort was made to combine traditional techniques with the new ideas of the Renaissance. This painting is by B. de Bruyn.

Nº 10.

Votive painting. Vertical panel, which appears to be part of a triptych. The composition follows the same principle as that of nº 8, though with greater simplicity. A bare stone wall is the intermediary between the figure in the foreground and the landscape, the perspective of which starts at the top of the wall. The head of the saint stands out against the ground of this landscape. This painting is the work of J.V. Melem.

RENAISSANCE.

RENAISSANCE

Schmidt, lith.

Imp. Firmin-Didot & Cie Paris

RENAISSANCE.

MANUSCRIPT ORNAMENTATION, XVIth–XVIIth CENTURIES.

THE ITALIAN STYLE OF THE HIGH RENAISSANCE.

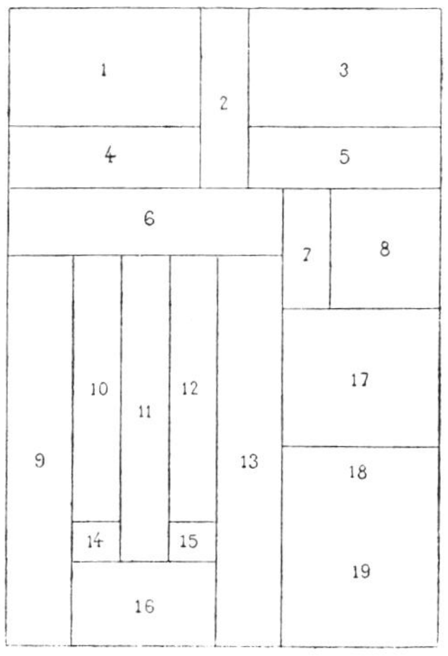

We would draw the reader's attention to the ingenuity of a broad-minded ornamentalist of this period who decorated with mostly pagan images the margins of a book essentially Christian in character: the missal of a cardinal contemporary of Leon X. A missal is a book containing the prayers, canon, and ceremonies of the mass. Those in holy orders were required to read this book, which served as a breviary, every day. Here, the artist has succeeded, without offending the beliefs of his client, in placing before his eyes a universe of images particularly pleasing to educated Italians of this period, who were so taken by the monuments of Antiquity, its numismatics, its intaglios, its cameos, and its legends.

Motifs Nos 1, 3, 4, 5, 7, 9, 10, 12, 13, 17 and 19 come from two pages of a missal which belonged to Cardinal Pompey Colonna, bishop of Montréal, and viceroy of Naples where he died in 1532. His arms (the column, to signify his name, Colonna) are represented in the central medallion of nos 1 and 3 with the cardinal's hat depicted above them. The inscription on n° 3 reads as follows: DIVO CARDINALE POMPEIO COLUMNE. This manuscript, n° 1, is from the Sciarra Library in Rome.

Pompey Colonna was one of those warrior priests who, like Pope Julius II, against whom he stirred up the Roman people in 1512, could be portrayed as Michelangelo's *Pensieroso*. In fact, he liked and protected men of letters and aspired to be of their number. A poem of his has survived, *de Laudibus mulierum*, dedicated to Vittoria Colonna.

Traditionally the illuminations of the Cardinal's missal are attributed to Raphael. This hypothesis is by no means confirmed, although the taste for small-scale ornamentation, the choice of motifs and their composition do recall, at times, the ornamental designs of the Loggia in the Vatican.

The creator of these margins and initials set out to summon up in his vignettes the pagan universe in which Christianity first originated and spread. Only in the openings of the initials, n°s 17 and 19, do Saint John and Saint Mathew appear, the Precursor and the Evangelist. This opening is like a window through which the new dawn will shine, in the radiance of which the old mythologies of Egypt, Greece and Rome are destined to fade.

In the remaining areas, architecture and statuary. medallions and cameos of characteristic subjects suggest the past, which was the present at the time of the Gospel. Monuments to the great divinities are combined with elements of a secondary order representing sphinxes and winged female monsters, chimeras, harpies, satyrs with cloven hoofs and tritons with a fish tail instead of legs, to complete the picture of a universe alive with fantastic creatures.

N°s 1, 4, 9 and 10 belong to the border of the same page; n° 4 is at the top, n° 5 serves as a base. The initial n° 17 is within this frame.

The cameos of motif n° 9 represent: at the top, *Venus tritonia*, in the middle, Daphne pursued by Apollo and transformed into a laurel, and at the bottom, the abduction of Ganymede. The subjects of the medallions are the abduction of Proserpina, and Medea in her chariot pulled by dragons.

The cameo in n° 10 represents Eros or Cupid, the god of love, son of Aphrodite and possibly of Aries or Mars, Zeus or Jupiter, or Hermes or Mercury, Venus having remained silent on the subject. The abduction of Europa and the metamorphosis into myrrh of Myrrha or Smyrna, the mother of Adonis, are the subjects of the medallions.

The central motif of n° 4 is a portrait, most probably of Augustus. On either side, a child riding a dolphin holds a weather vane in one hand, symbol of everchanging destiny.

In n° 1, tritons play with children, one of whom is holding a conch.

A naïad adorns n° 17, while in the initial Saint John is portrayed in traditional fashion, wearing a sheep skin, accompanied by a little lamb, and holding a fragile cross in his hand.

N°s 3, 5, 7, 12 and 13 are part of the same arrangement, along with the initial n° 19.

In n° 12, one can see a triumphal column in the style of the Trajan Column. Priapus is portrayed beneath it in the shape of a herm, with drapery. The small *tableaux* depict a sacrifice and the effigy of a ruler of Asian appearance. The structure is upheld by a crouching deity of Egyptian character.

At the top of n° 13, a desert lion is shown in profile. Beneath it is an obelisk covered with hieroglyphs and supported by sphinxes. Then there is a scene of hieratic appearance: Zeus or the shining sun, a river image, the Nile and its ibises, a Greek style structure, sanctuary of an Egyptian idol, accompanied by the rigid figures of deities with human bodies and animal heads, and finally, in a Greek cage, a figure, possibly Ptolemy, with a pharaonic appearance. N° 7, which is a fragment of the same page, depicts an Egyptian god with a human aspect. Apis the ox is shown in N° 5, along with the venerated cat, vases for sacrificial libations, and the bronze helmet or mitre with the *lituus* of kings. Sphinxes with human heads and the bodies of lions are depicted in motif n° 3.

The initial n° 19, inside which Saint Matthew appears writing his Gospel under the dictation of an angel, is adorned with the following motifs: Hercules suffocating Anteus, severing the contact between the latter and his mother, Earth, and Diana of Ephesus the huntress, Artemis to the Greeks, with her countless breasts to nurse all living creatures, the *multimammia* goddess, as she was named by Saint Jerome in his epistle to the Ephesians.

The small motif n° 2 which functions as a separation between two columns of text on the same page, and the initials n°s 14 and 15 are from the missal of Pope Pius II which is now in the Chigi Library in Rome. It was painted around 1450, and the margins of this manuscript are in a very different spirit from those of the missal of Colonna. They are composed of a series of small pictures showing scenes from the Holy Scriptures, the Gospel, and the Acts of the Apostles.

N°s 6, 8 and 16, borders and initials, are found in a manuscript of Pliny, the naturalist (Royal Library of Turin). These symmetrical, elegant and perfectly executed ornaments, date from the sixteenth century. The illustrations in this manuscript have no particular meaning.

N°s 11 and 18 are taken from the borders of the missal of Cardinal Cornaro, Minerva Library, Rome.

Frederic Cornaro, Bishop of Bergamo, was promoted to cardinal in 1670, during the pontificate of Clement X. He ordered the Chapel of Saint Teresa to be built at his expense, in Saint Mary of the Victory, after the drawings of Bernini. The ornamentation of this manuscript is marked by the freedom characteristic of the style of the period and its whimsical nature demonstrates the desire to part with tradition. Colourless foliage of the acanthus family produces natural colourful flowers. The spirit of the book is evoked by the monochrome medallions depicting prophets from the Old Testament or figures of saints. The charming colouring of the white foliage and the natural flowers against a golden or silver background prefigures the type of light-coloured decorations which were to reach their peak in the eighteenth century. However ordered this composition may be, a notable degree of fantasy is already present in these illustrated margins, the religious character of which is confined to the effigies in the medallions. The range of the paganism in the Colonna missal goes far beyond the gallant elegance of this style.

RENAISSANCE.

Bénard, lith
Imp. Firmin-Didot & Cie Paris

RENAISSANCE.

ORNAMENTATION OF MANUSCRIPTS. — XVth, XVIth CENTURIES.

THE USE OF GOLDWORK IN THEIR DECORATION.

With the exception of the initial in the middle of the page, this plate is made up of elements taken from a single source: *The Hours of Aragon*. These motifs are supplemented by borders taken from the same Italian manuscript and shown in the next plate, which bears the symbol of the *epaulet*. The character of these ornaments is more exclusively that of goldwork enriched with gems. In fifteenth- and early sixteenth-century Italy, young artists started out as apprentice goldsmiths. Artists like Brunellesco, Ghiberti, Donatello, Nasolino, and Lucca della Robbia, were no exception to this rule and they had learned to engrave jewellery and set precious stones before spreading their wings. The same is true of Mariotto Albertinelli, Andrea del Sarto, or Baccio Bandinelli, who, like their predecessors, were familiar with the secrets of this most refined of techniques, having learned to concentrate their skill, talent and imagination within the most minute frame so that these "apprentices" had become accomplished artisans before they took on the range and boldness of superior forms of art. The creator of the *Hours of Aragon* is of this school.

Alphonse, prince of Aragon, whose arms adorn the manuscript, was an amateur who took pleasure in supporting copyists and especially in commissioning manuscripts illuminated with freshness and brilliance, qualities he considered to be of utmost importance. He employed eight scribes, who were permanently occupied, two miniaturists and two bookbinders. The latter also used the techniques of the goldsmith to decorate the covers of their books. A specific binding was given to each book according to its category. In the Medici Library, sacred works were bound in blue, grammar books in yellow, poetry in purple, history in red, art books in green, and philosophy in white.

The initial D was painted by Monte di Giovanni di Favilla, who lived from 1492 to 1528, and spent many years working on the choir books of the Cathedral of Florence, from which this motif is taken. This artist was both a prominent mosaicist and a talented miniaturist. The commentators of Vasari have drawn parallels between his style and those of Van Eyck and Memling, under whom Monte and his brother, Gerard, are said to have worked.

At the top of the initial is a vase which contains blooming lily stems painted in natural colours, along with foliage in the conventional style. At the bottom, an angel holds a rich jewel made of pearls, amethysts and rubies, the radiance of which may symbolize the meaning of the saint's name which comes from Lux, meaning light. The jewel may also be a reminder of the vision which led to the vocation of this Christian woman: a dream of Saint Agatha amidst angels and adorned with precious stones.

With artists as educated as the Italians of Florence, it is often possible to find subtle meanings in their work. In any event, the sword piercing the martyr's neck indicates that this Saint Lucia is not the virgin of Bologna, who, to escape the obstinate persecutions of an admirer enamoured of her eyes, tore them out with her own hands and sent them to him on a platter.

Brandin, lith.

Imp. Firmin Didot & Cie. Paris

RENAISSANCE.

MANUSCRIPT PAINTING, XVth–XVIth CENTURIES.

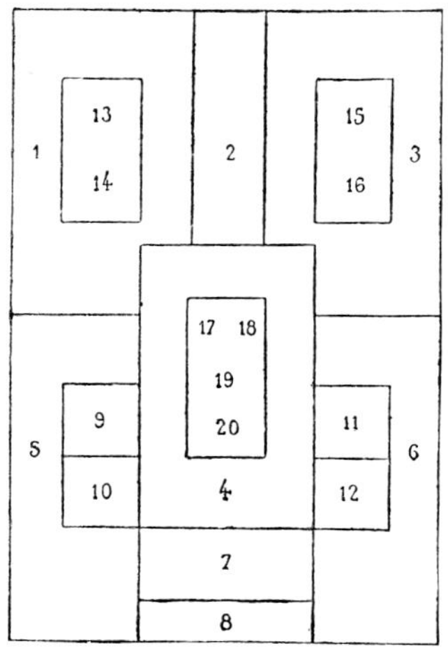

The frames shown on this plate are taken from the manuscript of the *Hours of Aragon*, so called because the arms of Aragon appear on the fourth page of the book. It is an Italian work of the sixteenth century and is now at the Bibliothèque nationale, nº 10,532, in Paris.

Nº 1.

Acanthus leafs are punctuated by florets painted in natural colours and real jewels arranged to look like fruits.

Nº 3.

The central scene on this page depicts the *Flagellation*, hence the basis of the marginal decorations, which is the thorn branch. The green of the foliage, the alternating red and white of the florets along with the sparkling jewels create a brilliant composition.

Nº 4.

The margin is decorated by an interplay of supple rush stems resembling Celtic interlace but with a wider openwork design. Here, jewellery is of lesser importance.

Nº 5.

Poppy leaves, alternately green and bronze in colour, with naturally coloured flowers decorate this margin, in which there are no jewels at all.

Nº 6.

There is one gem at the top of the page, the rest of the margin is adorned with pea pods and red potentilla flowers.

Nºs 7 and 8

Border fragments from the same manuscript. — Nº 7 is the base of an enamelled gold ornament. Its centre is marked by a splendid jewel. — Nº 8 is the top of a page decorated with oak branches laden with acorns, strawberries, and red potentilla flowers, against a lilac ground.

Decorated Letters.

Nº 9.

E. Initial taken from a *missale antiquum* in the public library of Lyon, painted in France, circa 1400.

Nº 10.

Another E, from the antiphonaries of the Charterhouse of Pavia. Brera Library, Milan.

Nº 11.

P. Same source as above.

Nº 12.

E. Saint John appears in the initial, wearing a sheep skin. Barberini Library, Rome.

Rosettes and Ornamental Motifs.

Nºs 13, 14, 15, 16, 17, 18, 19 and 20.

These details in the Gothic style are all taken from a *Gradual* belonging to the Cathedral of Siena and painted by Giovanni di Paolo, the Sienese.

Nº 2.

Fragment from the margin of a page where white and red bouquets of flowers alternate with each other, exemplifying a decorative scheme often used in the fifteenth century. The blossoming plant used in this ornamental technique looks as if it has just been uprooted, and it has little in common with the style of long stems sprinkled with florets or imaginary foliage fashioned according to the fancy of the artist.

RENAISSANCE

RENAISSANCE

Spiégel, lith.

Imp. Firmin-Didot & Cie, Paris

RENAISSANCE.

THE ARCHITECTURAL ORNAMENTATION OF PAINTED GLASS WINDOWS.

N° 6.

Border composed of a series of fleur-de-lis for Louis XII and ermines for Anne of Brittany, from a rose window, now destroyed, of the church of Gisors, 1500–15.

N°s 5, 7 and 8.

Motifs from the church of the Grand Andely, in Normandy, 1520. N° 5, with its architectural crown, is one of the most beautiful fragments of the Norman Renaissance. N° 7 is a fragment of the large rose window of the south transept. The elements of which this rose window is composed are similar to those of the window of the church of Gisors now destroyed. Two motifs are laid one on top of the other and repeated a great number of times, forming rays which converge towards the centre. N° 9 of the plate identified by the symbol of the *hand rattle* depicts the second motif, on the same green ground. Each of these motifs is trimmed with a running motif on a black background, n° 6. N° 8 is from the chapel of Saint-Christophe.

N°s 1, 3, 4 and 9

From the church of Saint-Vincent in Rouen, 1520–1530.

N° 2

From the church of Montmorency, 1535.

In the sixteenth century, stained-glass windows were common everywhere. They were found not only in royal palaces, churches or the dwellings of the powerful, but also in places of public assembly in all cities, and in oratories, cloisters, sitting rooms, private apartments, and so on. These stained-glass windows have little in common with those of the thirteenth, fourteenth and fifteenth centuries, either in terms of ornamental style or as regards method of execution. Prior to the sixteenth century, most of a stained-glass window was made up of glass that had been coloured in a piece. Only nude figures, white drapery and some parts of the background were painted on white glass. In the sixteenth century, however, the entire composition of a window came to be painted on plain glass. The use of enamel applied with a brush having become widespread during the fifteenth century, the similarities between this new technique and oil painting gradually gave rise to the idea of producing on glass effects similar to those obtained with oils. Hence the use of light tones, vigorous modelling, and deep perspectives, marking a departure from the principle of flat scenes which had been the rule for stained-glass compositions of the high Middle Ages. In windows made of pieces dyed in the molten glass, the whole takes precedence over detail while in sixteenth-century stained glass, the opposite is true. It is precisely the perfection of detail and the quality of draughtmanship and painting technique, largely inspired by the principles of the Italian Renaissance, which are innovative in this genre.

In France, the sixteenth-century artist in stained glass was trained in the school of the Italian Renaissance, because the reputation of French glass artists was such that they had been called to Italy during the pontificate of Julius II. The windows of the chapel of the Vatican were executed from sketches by Raphael by Master Claude and Brother Guillaume, both natives of Marseille. Furthermore, the school of Fontainebleau was a recognized authority in stained glass, represented by such artists as Jean Cousin and Bernard Palissy.

The general enthusiasm for the Italian style did not, however, completely annihilate the originality of French artists, and, in stained glass as well as in sculpture, several schools of the French Renaissance are discernible: the Norman school, the Parisian school and the school of Tours, for example. N° 2 in our plate, which is from Montmorency, is considered a product of both the Parisian school and the school of Tours. The elegance of the Norman school is of a different nature, as may be seen particularly in n°s 5 and 7.

Charpentier, lith

Imp. Firmin Didot & Cie. Paris

RENAISSANCE.

THE SCULPTURAL AND PICTORIAL ORNAMENTATION OF STAINED-GLASS WINDOWS.

THE WINDOW AS A WHOLE. — THE MASTERS OF THE PERIOD.

N°s 7, 9, 11 and 14.

From the church of the Grand Andely, in Normandy, 1515–1520. N° 7 is the fragment of a framing border from the chapel of Saint-Christophe. N° 6 is from the large rose window in the south transept, and goes with n° 7 of the plate identified by the symbol of the *table*. N° 14 is situated above a small door in the southern part of the church.

N° 8.

Ornament from the church of Saint-Patrice, in Rouen, 1520.

N° 2.

Panel from a chapel near the choir of the Cathedral of Rouen, dated 1521. This motif is characteristic of the Norman Renaissance.

N° 13.

Ornament from a window depicting Saint John the Baptist, in the church of Saint-Vincent, in Rouen, 1525–1526.

N° 12.

Frieze probably from the old church of Saint-Eloi, now in the archaeological museum of Rouen, 1530.

N° 10.

Keystone, depicted in the window of Saint-Crépin, from the church of Gisors, 1530.

N°s 1 and 3.

Canopies from the church of Montmorency, 1540 and 1535, respectively. N° 1 is at the top part of the window. This is a motif in the style of the school of Tours.

N° 4.

This fragment of painted architecture is part of a window in the church of Saint-Gervais in Paris. It is the work of Jean Pinaigrier, of the Parisian school, and is dated 1535.

N° 6.

Draped cartouche, from the ossuary of Saint-Etienne du Mont in Paris, 1535. This motif is one of the rare and final remnants of the Parisian Renaissance. This prototype points back to the painters of Fontainebleau and it was this style that was copied by artists under Louis XIII.

N° 5.

Part of a stained-glass window from the nave of the church of Saint-Patrice in Rouen, 1550.

These motifs are the continuation of the series shown in the previous plate, identified by the symbol of the *table*, and were sketched from the originals.

During the period when Guillaume and Claude were called from Marseille to Italy by Julius II, Arnaud de Moles, of whom almost nothing is known, created a series of stained-glass windows for the cathedral of Auch, which are its principal ornament. The inscription on a window in one of the side chapels, which has rescued the name of the artist from oblivion, is in Gascon dialect, suggesting that the master was a native of the Langudoc. It reads: LE XXV DE JVHN MIL V CENS XIII FON ACABADES LAS PRESENS BERINES EN AVNOVR DE DIOV ET DE NOSTD–ARNAUD DE MOLES ("On June 25, 1513 the present windows were completed to the honour of God and of Our Lady–Arnaud de Moles").

RENAISSANCE.

RENAISSANCE

Dreux, lith.

Imp. Firmin-Didot & Cie Paris

RENAISSANCE.

SCULPTURE. — TAPESTRY AND PAINTED WINDOWS. — FRENCH SCHOOLS.

THE ORNAMENTAL FIGURE IN THE HEROIC STYLE.

Most of the present documents complement the preceding plates, identified by the symbols of the *table* and the *hand-rattle*, a series concerned with sixteenth-century stained glass. Fragments taken from polychrome sculptures and tapestries of the same period have also been included in this illustration so that one may compare the different uses of colour from one medium to another.

N° 1 represents the top of the niches in the upper part of the tomb of the cardinals of Amboise, in the Cathedral of Rouen. This monument, one of the masterpieces of the Norman Renaissance, dates from 1520–40. It was executed by a colony of artists who had worked in the château of Gaillon from 1501 to 1509, in the château of Chenonceaux from 1515 to 1520, and on the choir of the Cathedral of Chartres. The project was directed by Rouland Leroux, master builder of the cathedral.

Nos 5 and 7. — Tapestry. Corner cartouche and cartouche from the running border of a hanging, the main subject of which is a Triumph. This tapestry is part of a series known as the Artemisia cycle, for which the sketches were revised several times in the course of the ninety years (1570 to 1660) it took for the royal shops of Paris to produce ten series of them. Thus, although cartouche n° 7 bears the monogram of Marie de Médicis, married to Henry IV in 1600, this does not necessarily indicate the date of the design. The figure seated in the corner, the sketch of which we believe to be among the early ones, can therefore be considered a product of the Fontainebleau school.

N° 19 is the design on the back of an armchair seen in an exhibition, along with nos 5 and 7, at the Palais des Champs-Elysées in 1876.

STAINED-GLASS WINDOWS.

Norman School.

1515. — N° 14. Church of Grand-Andely.

1520. — Nos 6, 10, 11, 15 and 17. Same church.

1520–1525. — Nos 16 and 18. Church of Saint Vincent, in Rouen.

1530. — Nos 2, 3, 9 and 13. Archeological museum of Rouen.

1535–1540. — N° 8. Church of Grand-Andely.

1560. — N° 4. Same church.

Parisian School.

Uncertain date. — N° 12. Church of Saint-Etienne du Mont. This motif of a very delicate design is reduced here to approximately two-thirds of the original size.

RENAISSANCE. RENAISSANCE. RENAISSANCE

Waret, del. Imp. Firmin-Didot & Cie Paris

RENAISSANCE.

ENAMELLED TERRACOTTA. — APPLIQUÉ DECORATION.

PAINTED SCROLLWORK ON CERAMIC AND STAINED GLASS.

ITALY, XVTH–XVITH CENTURY. — FRANCE, XVITH CENTURY.

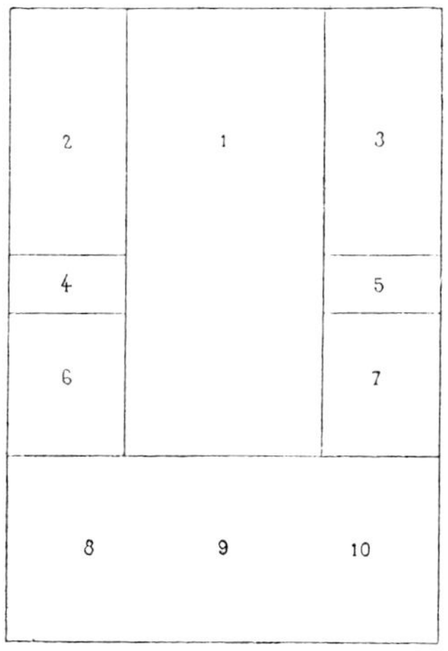

N° 1.

Architectonic ornament. Enamelled terracotta from the Louvre Museum. Works of this genre are called Tabernacles. In the original, this bas-relief is 1.66 metres in height and 0.65 metres in width. It is attributed to Luca the Younger. It reflects the techniques developed by Luca della Robbia, the head of the family, and the master of this fifteenth-century style.

At the centre of this piece, stands the door of the tabernacle, topped by an openwork oculus. Two haloed angels with clasped hands are bowed on either side of this door while the Holy Ghost, in the form of a dove, hovers above the oculus. The background is decorated with an arch in perspective, a compartmentalized ceiling and two raised curtains. The head of a cherub occupies both tympana. The two pilasters decorated with grotesques which frame this principal motif support an entablature, the frieze of which is decorated with the haloed heads of five cherubs. Above the cornice there is a scallop shell framed by an arched vault with palmettes on each side of its base. A chalice stands on the shell, supporting the Christ Child. Two small angels are bowed on either side. The entire structure is supported on a cornice held up by two cornucopias and decorated with a pelican feeding its young in a nest.

N°s 4, 5, 6 and 7

Decorative motifs on tiles from the Caffagiolo factory which was the main centre for Tuscan ceramics. Early sixteenth century.

N° 8.

Faience decorated in *sopra bianco*, which consists of white enamel designs against a slightly tinted white ground. This technique was rarely used alone. In our example, a regular green ornamental border adds colour to the composition. *Sopra bianco* decoration was mostly practised in Faenza and Urbino.

N° 9.

Ornamental scroll from a porcelain dish. It was in Florence that translucent pottery was first produced in Europe, the work, according to Vasari, of Bernardo Buontalenti. In fact, *porcellana* was not pure kaolin porcelain. The results were uneven: at times the paste had a greyish tinge or was yellowed by the firing, or else the enamel was not evenly glazed. Monochrome decoration, such as that illustrated made with pure cobalt, was rarely intense in tone or evenly applied overall. Nevertheless, the porcelain of the Medici, which is considered the best in Europe, was a true marvel for the period. Venice, Ferrara, Pesaro and Turin also developed their own porcelain. The dish reproduced here is decorated with nicely interwoven Italian-style scrollwork trimmed with a kind of band in a style of Oriental appearance.

N° 10.

Majolica. The name of Italian tin-glazed pottery with metallic reflections, majolica, comes from Majorca, one of the Balearic Islands, where Moorish craftsmen were believed to have developed this technique. However, the origin of this process, both in Spain and Italy, is now considered to lie in Far Eastern techniques, especially those of Persian ceramics. In Italy, this genre produced true marvels in the art of earthenware.

The dish shown here is reminiscent of majolica at a time when this technique was no longer practiced, either at Gubbio or Urbino. It dates from circa 1540.

Motifs n°s 2 and 3

From painted windows of the Norman Renaissance. This *grisaille* ornamentation against yellow grounds dates from 1530. N° 2 is located in the upper part of the choir of the church of Grand-Andely. N° 3 is from a window in the church of Gisors.

RENAISSANCE. RENAISSANCE.

Brandin, lith. Imp. Firmin Didot & Cie Paris

XVIth CENTURY.

GLAZED FAIENCE. — PAVEMENTS AND WALL-FACINGS.

Tiles for wall-facings, which cannot be used to cover floors, occupy the upper part of this plate. They are from Spain, dating presumably from the reign of Charles V and most probably executed by Italian craftsmen. These are delicate bas-reliefs, perfectly executed and exhibiting great purity of design. Two samples at the top of the plate offer examples of the effect obtained by assembling four tiles. The motif at the centre of the page is a single tile, reproduced on a slightly larger scale than the others in order to emphasize the beauty of composition. These tiles are in the museum of Limoges.

The motif on the lower part of the plate is a fragment of the pavement tiles at the foot of a hearth in a private mansion in Paris. These glazed faience tiles are of Italian origin. The combination of hexagonal and square shapes produces a lavish composition.

Daumont lith. Imp. Firmin Didot & Cie. Paris

RENAISSANCE.

ORNAMENTATION OF THE WAINSCOTS IN THE GALLERY OF FRANCIS I.

FONTAINEBLEAU PALACE.

The ornamentation of these beautiful panels is arranged around a central cartouche. The origin and function of the cartouche is expounded in the note accompanying the plate which bears the symbol of the *pulley*. The salamander of Francis I figures at the centre of the medallions. The variety and elegance of these compositions combining the motif of the cartouche with the use of ornamental scrollwork is particularly worthy of interest and demonstrates the skill of the Italian artists in softening the cartouche, adorning it with acanthus and other motifs drawn from Antiquity. The ornamental cartouche and the great number of possibilities it affords are not found in the art of Antiquity. While borrowing from Antiquity, the Renaissance of the sixteenth century thus created a decorative style of its own, which is neither Greek nor Roman.

The motifs on this plate are reproduced from photographic documents.

RENAISSANCE.

RENAISSANCE.

P. Lestel, lith.

Imp. Firmin-Didot & Cie Paris

RENAISSANCE.

SCULPTURED, PAINTED AND WOVEN CARTOUCHES,

XVIth–XVIIth CENTURIES.

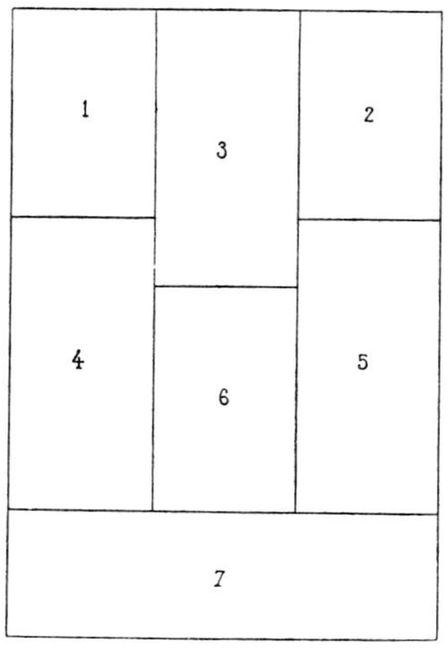

In principle, the ornamental cartouche is like a *monstrance* — that is, a case which served to house relics — it displays an inscription, a symbol, historical or mythological effigies, within an ornamental frame of varying complexity, enriched by all sorts of foliage, figures of every kind, flowers, fruit, ribbons, and so on. Often, a principal cartouche generates, as it were, smaller cartouches which tie in with the whole. At times, the cartouche is an ornament which is part of the architecture, while at others it is itself an imaginary and independent construction within the field bounded by the rim of a panel, or it decorates part of an unlimited field, taking on an airy lightness.

The simplest cartouche is the one to which the genre owes its name. The Romans wrote archives and books on strips of paper which were rolled to be stored in the *Bibliotheca*, as the Egyptians had done with papyrus. This paper, or vellum, was called *carta*. Unrolled, the *carta* or *charta* had a tendency to revert to its original position, and coiled up into scrolls at either end. The *carta* was still used in the Middle Ages for important documents, and the written challenge to a duel acquired the name of *cartel*. The decorated cartel is in fact the origin of the various fashions of ornamental cartouche.

The chivalrous cartel was frequently used in recreational battles such as tournaments. The heraldic shield was presented on a challenging cartel, sometimes designating a proposed adversary. It is assumed that the Germans were the first to use a cartel bearing a shield as an ornamental motif. Primarily using wood, their woodwork was carved to simulate the effects of the flexible carta, with accidental tears which coil up to form whimsical irregular scrolls, the asymmetry of which did not suit the taste of the Italians. The latter, recognizing the advantages of this genre, extended its application by adapting its construction to the object or area to be decorated, using high and low relief so as to subordinate the architectural cartouche, which remained symmetrical, to the necessities of the whole. Following their example, the cartouche motif became widely used in France, Spain and Flanders, and it was only under the influence of Bernini that, in the last part of the seventeenth century, the asymmetrical cartouche reappeared. It was to reach its peak in the eighteenth century, when the fashion for all things Chinese flourished.

N[os] 1 and 2 are from the gallery of Francis I, in the Fontainebleau Palace. These fragments make up the two ends of a long architectural cartouche which follows the principle of the *carta*, a flat surface with scrolls on either end, folded backwards. This wall decoration is skillfully conceived to combine painting and sculpture. The fold of the *carta* hides the thickness of the wall, softening the angles of the windows where the ornament ends, and allows for the positioning of two caryatids. To remedy the bareness of the genre, a smaller cartouche has been added, decorated with a bas-relief and following the same principle as the larger one. The scrolled carta serves as a support for the caryatids. Another cartouche occupies the upper part of these fragments, this one in the style of joinery, displaying a basket of flowers and smaller figures in relief.

The superb gallery of Francis I was executed from the drawings and under the supervision of Il Rosso, the Florentine painter and architect. He also designed the ornaments themselves, the reliefs and *bas-reliefs*, the execution of which was carried out by the Italian sculptor, Paolo Ponzio. It was not until after Il Rosso's death that Primaticcio added to the borders and various ornaments of this gallery. Giovanni Battista del Rosso, the true founder of the School of Fontainebleau, was born in Florence in 1496 and died in Paris in 1541. He had been especially influenced by the work of Jules Romain (Giulio Pippi) in the Te Palace in Mantua.

N[os] 1 and 2 include colossal caryatids of stucco whose function as supports is more illusory than real, unlike the Greek style where the effigies of slaves replaced the columns in supporting the weight of a temple. Their use was based on the contempt of the Hellenes for the women of Caria, who had given their name to a style which already existed among the Egyptians and Assyrians. Here, the caryatids give movement to the rigid structure of the cartouche. Being purely decorative, they need only give the illusion of supporting the structure and their figures need not be immobile and upright, as those of classical caryatids.

This mural decoration is completed by a wainscot which serves as the basis for the large sculptured and painted cartouche. (See the plate identified by the symbol of the *claws*, for the detail of these wood carvings.)

N[os] 6 and 7 are border fragments from a tapestry. The cartouches, fastened to mouldings, are tied in with the architectural design. Again, they follow the principle of the scrolled carta, however the central part is no longer flat. A medallion, set in a gilded border, serves as a monstrance. Furthermore, the carta is now of double or triple thickness in layers which are linked one to another. Both of these are fragments from two tapestries which belong to the series of hangings known as the Artimesia series, the borders of which were executed around 1610, in the royal workshops of Henry IV. The design of these ornaments, however, is of an earlier date, when the royal shops first started work on this cycle of tapestries, in 1570.

N[os] 3, 4 and 5 complete the motifs shown on the plate identified by the symbol of the *tub*. The caption to that plate provides details regarding the decoration of door panels. N[o] 3 is dedicated to Henry IV and bears his portrait. Above the portrait, a personification of Glory blows the Trumpet of Fame while, below, the ship of State is occupied by two men holding the royal attributes: a *fleur-de-lis* sceptre and the hand of justice.

N° 4 shows the interwoven monograms of Anne of Austria and Louis XIII with the following epigraph: *Ad spem, spes addita Gallis* ("New hope united to the hope of France"). The motto in n° 5, above the effigy of Marie de Medici, reads: *Numquam sub mole fatiscit* ("she does not succumb under the burden").

N°s 1, 2, 3, 4, and 5 are reproduced from photographs. N°s 6 and 7 were shown in an exhibition of tapestries organized by the Union centrale des arts décoratifs in 1876.

Charpentier lith.

Imp. Firmin-Didot & Cie Paris.

XVIIth CENTURY.

DECORATIVE PAINTINGS. — FONTAINEBLEAU PALACE.

Because of the excellent quality of these decorations, the style of which is compatible with works from the times of Henry IV and Louis XIII, we have chosen to include them among the decorative painting of the early seventeenth century. In actuality, these emblematic medallions, from the wainscotting of the first of the reception apartments in the Fontainebleau Palace, were executed under the direction of Moench, a decorative painter, who, in 1834, had been entrusted by Louis-Philippe with the task of restoring the *Salle des Gardes*.

The information necessary to reconstruct the original ornamentation was still in existence: fragments of the cartoons for the ceiling, which was in tatters, were discovered under the canvas covering it and showed the designs and colours, the trophies and remnats of arms painted in oil on a golden ground. However scattered these fragments of information may have been, it was relatively easy to recreate the ceiling and the frieze as they were at the time of Louis XIII. The wainscotting was given a richly coloured decoration against a white background.

Five doors, real or illusory, of the *Salle des Gardes* were decorated with double panels commemorating the sovereigns who had been involved in the extension or embellishment of the Palace of Fontainebleau. These include Francis I, Henry II, Anthony of Bourbon, father of Henry IV, Henry IV himself, Louis XIII and, naturally Louis-Philippe, the reigning king. The panels offer an ingenious summary of the history of each of these men through allegorical figures, emblems, mottoes, and so on.

The two large panels are part of the decoration of the third door, to the left of the chimney, which is dedicated to Anthony of Bourbon, duke of Vendôme. They depict, on one side, the portrait of the hero of Les Andelys, with the arms of Vendôme, and on the other, the anagram of Jeanne d'Albret, with the arms of Navarre. Two panels with the interwoven initials of Henry IV and Marie de Medici display emblems, each with a different motto: *Umbra lux recta fugat* ("His righteous light dissipates shadows") and *Fulgenti diademate partus* ("Child of a radiant diadem"). Finally, the motto of the small lower central panel, bearing the initials of Anne of Austria, reads as follows: *Aquilis generosior ales* ("A bird more generous than eagles").

Charpentier lith.

Imp. Firmin Didot & Cie Paris

RENAISSANCE.

LIMOGES ENAMELS, GRISAILLES.

Nos 1, 12, 16 and 17.

Motifs taken from a stemmed dish with a lid. N° 1 is actually made up of two motifs. The motif with a medallion showing a child on the back of a dolphin is the interior decoration of the dish, while the area around the circle above the medallion shows the exterior ornamentation of the lid. N° 12 is an egg-and-dart border. N° 16 is the decoration on the stem, while N° 17 shows the inner border of the lid of this dish, which was made by Pierre Reymond.

Nos 2 and 14.

Fragments from the decoration of a round dish, by the same master. N° 2: the inside of the dish. N° 14: its underside.

N° 3.

Exterior decoration of a stemmed dish by Jehan Court.

Nos 4, 11 and 15.

Interior ornamentation of a dish by P. Courteys. Nos 4 and 15 belong to this one motif with a variety of grotesque masks.

Nos 9 and 10.

Decoration of a circular dish by P. Reymond who signed it with his initials in one cartouche and the date 1558 in another. N° 9 is the border of the back of the dish.

N° 5.

Fragment of the ornamentation of the stem of a dish, by the same artist.

N° 6.

Border on a small enamelled chest.

Nos 7 and 8.

Fragments of the decoration of an ewer. N° 7 is painted on the inside of the neck. N° 8 is divided into two parts. The top fragment is from the ornamentation of the lower part of the vase, while the lower motif is taken from the ornaments of the stem. The enamelist is P. Courteys.

Pierre Reymond was most probably born in the early years of the sixteenth century. The earliest date found on his works is 1534. He was active until 1584, that is for approximately fifty years. He reached the height of his powers around 1550.

Pierre Courteys, who signs his name P. Corteys, Courteys, Cortoys, Courtoys and Corteu, was active at around the same period. The earliest dates found on his enamels are 1545 and 1548. The last is 1568. It appears that he was trained in the workshop of Pierre Reymond.

Jehan Court, known as Vigier, of whom few works have survived, is an enamellist who belongs to the great period of the French Renaissance. The only dates found on his enamels are 1556 and 1557. His style is more sober than those of P. Reymond and P. Courteys.

Around the year 1520, the traditional technique of painting on a painted surface was almost entirely abandoned by the enamellists of Limoges. They turned to what is called *grisaille*, although the old method was still sometimes used to vary the effects of the monochrome *grisaille*.

In all the *grisailles* of the sixteenth century, a line silhouettes the various elements of the subject, lending firmness to the draughtmanship. This, coupled with the relative modesty of the modelling, is what confers such a pronounced decorative character on these enamels.

The abuse of golden spangles and golden highlights eventually compromised the artistic value of the products of Limoges, to the extent that their prices fell significantly by the end of the sixteenth century.

Brandin, lith.

Imp. Firmin-Didot & Cie. Paris.

RENAISSANCE.

LIMOGES GRISSAILLES. — THE DECORATION OF COUNTER-ENAMELS.

EMBROIDERIES AND PAINTINGS.

Enamels.

N° 3.

Reverse side of an oval dish. Decoration of a counter-enamel, signed with a monogram, I.C., the initials of Jehan Courteys, to whom this piece is attributed.

This enameller, who never dated his works, is presumed to have lived in Limoges in 1545, and died in 1586, leaving a son by the same name. It is often difficult to distinguish the works of Jehan Courteys from those of Jehan de Court, who signed his pieces with the same monogram. Both were active in the second half of the sixteenth century.

"One thing that must not be ignored", says the *Encyclopedia* of the eighteenth century, under *Enamel*, "is that every piece enamelled *en plein* on the side which is to be painted, must be counter-enamelled on the other side, with half as much enamel if it is convex; if it is level, the same quantity is necessary for the counter-enamel as for the enamel. One begins with the counter-enamel."

The function of counter-enamel, or the enamelling of the reverse side of the metal, was to avoid a piece becoming twisted during the firing process. It was indispensable and as such was often more or less apparent according to the shape of a piece. The ornamentation of counter-enamels was quite varied and contributed significantly to the richness of this sumptuous industry. In some cases both sides of a work will have similar decorations: a *grisaille* with gold highlights on a brown background, for example, as in the case of the plates from the shops of Léonard Limosin. In others, the reverse side contrasts with the principal decorative style of the work.

Several of the motifs displayed in our plate identified by the symbol of the *parasol* are, in fact, counter-enamel decorations.

N°s 4 and 5.

Repeating motifs from the borders of dishes in the style of Léonard Limosin.

Léonard was one of the greatest and most famous enamellers of Limoges. He was from a Limosin family, seven members of which devoted their lives to the art of enamelling. In his first works, Léonard was influenced primarily by the German masters. In 1532, he produced plaques in the manner of Albrecht Dürer and copied prints by Raphael. It is, however, to the Fontainebleau school, and especially to the works of Nicolo dell'Abbate, who had joined the school in 1552, that Léonard owes the style of his best productions.

Both our examples, in fact, are in the manner of Nicolo dell'Abbate. The design is somewhat mannered in the exaggeration of muscles, the slenderness of joints, and the elongation of proportions in the figures. However, the sense of freedom in these motifs is remarkable and the beautiful movement of the figured foliage is typical of the ample and independent style of Léonard Limosin.

The latest dated works of Léonard Limosin, born circa 1505, are from 1574.

N°s 6, 7 and 14.

Fragments from objects in the style of Pierre Courteys. N°s 6 and 7 are from the stem of a stemmed dish. N° 14 is from the upper part of an ewer. N° 8 of the plate identified by the symbol of the *parasol* is taken from the same piece.

The latest known works by Pierre Courteys are dated 1568. His style, no longer inspired by the school of Fontainebleau, is of lesser artistic interest though it is richer in finely executed details. This manner is close to that of goldsmiths such as François Briot or Etienne de Laulne who were very much in favour during the reign of Henry II.

N° 8 is a mask from the underside of a dish by Pierre Rémond, while N° 11 is a grotesque which completes the series of four such ornaments, three of which are depicted in the previous plate (n°s 2, 11 and 15).

Embroideries and paintings.

N°s 1 and 2.

Corner motifs, taken from the illumination of manuscripts. They are the work of Girolamo da Cremona and are found in the choir books of the cathedral of Florence, fifteenth century.

N°s 9 and 10.

Of a similar character. Witty fragments by Liberale da Verona. Antiphonary of the cathedral of Siena.

N°s 12 and 13.

Ground and border of a tapestry from the canopy of a chair. Second half of the sixteenth century.

N° 15.

Continuous fabric pattern dating from the reign of Henry II.

N° 16.

Tunic border, same period.

These details, taken from tapestries, were displayed in an exhibition organized in Paris by the Union centrale des arts décoratifs in 1876. The Limoges enamels are from a private collection, recently donated to Russia.

RENAISSANCE

RENAISSANCE. RENAISSANCE

Brandin, lith

Imp. Firmin Didot & Cie. Paris

XVIth CENTURY.

ORNAMENTAL FOLIAGE. — FLEMISH TAPESTRIES.

In point of fact, one can say of the tapestries of Flanders that they are the European tapestry of the sixteenth century. In terms of ornamentation, they demonstrate the purest and most straightforward expression of the Italian Renaissance.

In the sixteenth century, Flemish craftsmen brought the tapestry industry to Florence, Ferrara and Mantua as well as to Spain, Bavaria and England. As for France, though tapestry manufactories existed in several cities in the Middle Ages, in Beauvais and Reims in particular, the creation of the first workshops in Aubusson and Felletin is attributed to a colony of Flemish artisans. Francis I had attempted, in fact, to establish in Fontainebleau a tapestry factory under the direction of Primaticcio but it did not last, and this project, taken over by Henry II and Catherine de Medici, left few traces. It was Henry IV who, by establishing a high-warp factory, which moved from the place Royale to the neighbourhood of the Gobelins around 1630 and the first factory of velvet weavings in the Louvre, set the national industry in motion. The tapestries from the Gobelins manufactory, established by Colbert in 1662, were to earn great renown.

The ornamentation of sixteenth-century Flemish tapestries is marked by the influence of the Italian style of the Renaissance and has little in common with the styles of the Middle Ages.

Our examples are fragments from anonymous works. However, cartoons by great artists were often the model for Flemish tapestries, and hangings were woven in Brussels from drawings by Mantegna, Raphael, Jules Romain, or Albrecht Dürer.

N°s 1, 2 and 4 are fragments of the same border. The figures are similar to those on the reverse side of an enamelled dish from Limoges (n° 3, symbol of the *chalice*). However, the ornamentation here is richer and lighter. It is nevertheless probable that the two motifs date from the same period, that is, the second half of the sixteenth century.

N°s 3, 6, 7 and 9 are also motifs borrowed from borders.

In the beautiful Italian cartoons, the ornamentation often extends to the costumes of the figures as well as the objects and furnishings of the central scene. The luxury of this type of detail dates back to the school of Mantegna. Among the motifs of the Renaissance, these are the most clearly reminiscent of Antiquity.

N°s 5, 8, 10 and 11 are of this nature. In the original, n° 5 adorns the top of a tunic; n° 8 is the decoration on a legging; n° 10 is the trimming of a tunic; n° 11, finally, is the decoration on a flower vase.

Schmidt, lith

Imp. Firmin Didot & Cie, Paris

XVIth CENTURY.

THE ORNAMENTATION OF OFFENSIVE WEAPONS.

ENAMELLED STEEL. — CHASING.

The hilts of a sword and dagger presented here are made of steel and decorated with *cloisonné* enamels on a gold background, as are their scabbards and swordbelts. Weapons decorated in such a fashion are rare. These specimens dating from the reign of Henry II (1547–59) were part of a collection acquired by Napoleon III and are now in the Museum of Artillery in Paris. The length of the original pieces is 1.20 metres for the sword, and 0.34 metres for the dagger.

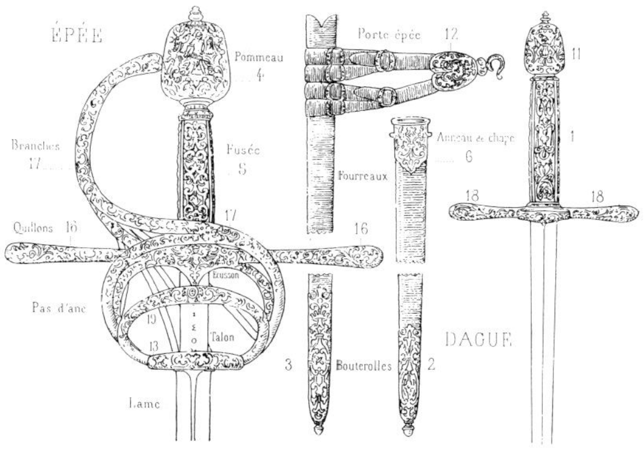

We have included above drawings of the two hilts and scabbards in order to make plain the details shown in the plate which, in some cases, have had to be flattened out. These details are cross-referenced by number.

N° 4.

Flattened motif on the pommel of the sword.

N° 5.

One of the sides of the tang.

N° 16.

Ornamentation of the quillons including the escutcheon.

N° 17.

Decoration of the branch, flattened.

N° 19.

Middle part of the protective guard.

N° 13.

Lower part of the protective guard.

N° 11.

Flattened motif on the pommel of the dagger.

N° 1.

One of the sides of the tang.

N° 18.

Ornamentation of its quillons.

N° 15.

Ornamentation of the guard.

Ornamentation of scabbards

N°s 9, 10 and 12.

Hook of the sword frog.

N° 3.

Chape of the scabbard of the sword.

N°s 7, 8, 14.

Swordbelt buttons.

N° 6.

Chape ring from the scabbard of the dagger.

N° 2.

Its chape.

Spiégel, lith. Imp. Firmin Didot & Cie, Paris.

XVIth–XVIIth CENTURY.

MANUSCRIPT ORNAMENTATION IN ITALY.

SECOND HALF OF THE XVITH CENTURY.

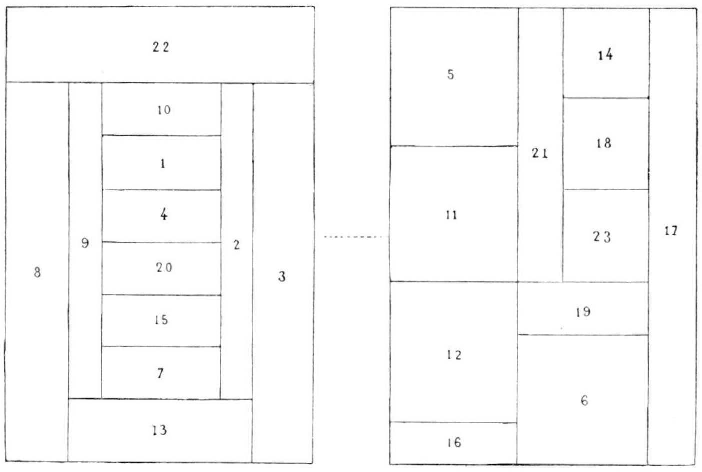

The elements of this plate and of the following one, identified by the symbol of the *buckle*, are from a single source: the *Antiphonaries* of the Charterhouse of Pavia, now kept in the Brera Library in Milan. These choir books are of particular interest when considering the history of the evolution of ornamental styles, as the execution of these fourteen volumes spanned many years. Indeed, the date 1562 is found in the third volume while one ornament of the twelfth volume is dated 1578. Thus, it is reasonable to assume that work was started on these volumes prior to the first date and continued well after the second. In fact, by their style, the examples taken from the thirteenth and fourteenth volumes proclaim the end of the sixteenth century and the dawn of the seventeenth. On the other hand, the early illustrations in these manuscripts undoubtedly reflect the influence of the Charterhouse of Pavia, built from 1396 to 1542, which was magnificently decorated by the master goldsmiths of Milan. Among these we shall name only Cardosso, sculptor, goldsmith, enameller, whose influence was strongly felt in Rome.

The motifs shown on the two plates (identified by the symbols of the *chain* and the *buckle*) have been numbered in chronological order.

N° 1. — Volume 2. — Motif borrowed from the first page. The portrait is that of Giovanni Visconti, founder of the Charterhouse of Pavia.

N°s 2, 3 and 4. — Volume 3. — The two vertical borders face each other on the page. The date of 1562 is shown in the medallion at the centre of the wider of the two borders. The corresponding small medallion bears the monogram of

Christ. This ornamental composition is based on the principle of classical fountains and candelabras.

N°s 5 and 6. — Volume 6. — Initials N and D. The tendency towards elaboration is most obvious in the letter D, which is of lesser artistic value and painted backwards. by mistake. In both of these letters, the inner scene appears to have been covered up. Whatever the reason, it is clear that this was done at a later date. The inner decoration of the N is seventeenth-century.

N°s 7, 8, 9 and 10. — Volume 10. — The uprights n°s 8 and 9 are of the same nature as those we have already seen. The wider of the two motifs is purely ornamental, with no added human figures, while in the narrow band facing it, two small figures play the drum. The medallion at the centre of the latter motif bears the date of 1565. The medallion in nº 10 depicts the Saviour lamenting the sins of the world. This style of ornamentation belongs to the art of enamelling.

N°s 11, 12, 13 and 14. — Volume 12. — The ornamentation, executed by a superior draughtsman, of the initial nº 11 is truly new in character. The scene inside the letter represents Ezekiel holding a tablet with the following biblical inscription: "Therefore prophesy, and say unto them, Thus saith the Lord God, Behold, O my people, I will open your graves, and cause you to come out from your graves, and bring you into the land of Israel" (Ezek. 37:12).

Nº 12 is an I, the ornamentation of which does not include an inner scene. This purely decorative and whimsical motif includes figures, painted in natural colours: children playing with birds, and female torsos with the ears and pear-shaped breasts of female fauns, stemming from the foliage.

Nº 13, dated 1578, is in a more innovative style, and of better taste. The composition and colouring of this motif is indeed so different from the others that it was probably the work of an artist from a school other than the Milanese school, possibly that of Bologna. The entire border of this page exhibits this style of ornamentation.

The initial nº 14, with its inner scene, is in a more conventional style.

N°s 15, 16, 17 and 18. — Volume 13. — Elegance and grace in movement of symmetrical fantasy are the principle aim of the ornamentation of n°s 15 and 16. The evidence of a new spirit is obvious here. The elements of this new style are evident in nº 17 but the most felicitous example of it is our exquisite motif nº 15.

N°s 19, 20, 21, 22 and 23. — Volume 14. — Nº 22 most clearly illustrates a new opulence, with the use of the cartouche which stands unadorned. As in nº 20, the figures, when there are any, accompany the cartouche and are part of the decoration surrounding it. In example nº 22, the figures supporting the cartouche present it in the spirit of the true cartel. In fragment nº 21, creatures and figures are depicted within a tumultuous foliated scroll, at the base of which are three child musicians.

Nº 19, finely executed, recalls a style favoured by the Greeks in which two separate identical scrolls mirror each other. The sobriety of this style and its fidelity to classical principles stands in contrast with the movement we have just seen and foreshadows serious artists such as Nicolas Poussin.

Nº 23 is an O, inside which Saint Sebastian is depicted tied to a tree and pierced with an arrow. The letter itself forms a cartouche and the subject of the scene has inspired the shaping of this cartouche which includes two wooden bows. None of the initials in earlier volumes of the *Antiphonary* exhibit a similar feature and the ornamentation of the present fragment thus marks the emergence of a triumphant genre. The prevailing influence at the time was Flemish.

Gaulard lith.

Imp. Firmin Didot & Cie Paris

XVIth–XVIIth CENTURY.

ORNAMENTATION OF MANUSCRIPTS IN ITALY.

SECOND HALF OF THE XVIth CENTURY.

We have reproduced below the plans showing the numeration of the motifs distributed between the plates identified by the symbols of the *chain* and the *buckle*, along with a summary of the volumes these examples are taken from. Details regarding these illustrations are included in the caption accompanying the previous plate.

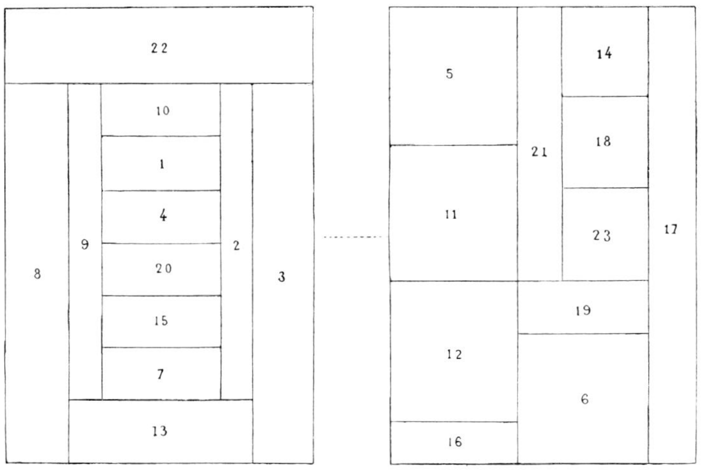

Gaulard, lith. Imp. Firmin-Didot & Cie Paris

RENAISSANCE.

ORNAMENTATION OF MANUSCRIPTS. — CARTOUCHES IN WOOD.

This page and the border fragments which accompany it are drawn from one source, *La Vie des ducs d'Urbin* (The Lives of the Dukes of Urbino), a manuscript in the Library of the Vatican, in Rome.

The ornamentation displayed in our plate combines two separate elements. On the one hand, the ornamental scrolls and the superimposing of motifs in vertical pannels were inspired by Roman Antiquity. On the other, the cartouches, — those constructions which form a distinct element and are either isolated or worked in with the rest of the ornamentation, — were developed during the Renaissance and do not have classical equivalents. In subsequent centuries, the place these cartouches were to take in both architectural and pictorial decoration is of such importance that it is possible to determine the date of a particular decorative work according to the style of its cartouches.

The large cartouche serving as a frame for the portrait of the Duke Francesco Maria I is characteristic of an early style of cartouche which has the appearance of carved wood. Durcereau and especially Théodore de Bry, in his remarkable Alphabet, fragments of which are shown in the following pages, produced excellent examples of this style.

In the original, the portrait is a miniature painted in full colour. The tree depicted in a medallion recalls the oak of the arms of the della Rovere of Urbino.

RENAISSANCE

Charpentier, lith.

Imp. Firmin Didot & Cie. Paris

XVIth CENTURY.

CONSTRUCTED ORNAMENT.

FRAMES, CARTOUCHES AND FLEURONS.

In its variety, the form of ornamentation based on finely carved woodwork which is given the appearance of a logical construction while still allowing all sorts of additions, such as flowers, fruits, figures, and so on, is the expression of an art specifically European in character.

The movement which produced this genre coincides with the propagation of the Italian Renaissance, however the features of these delicate constructions by no means belong to classical Antiquity. Particularly in the cartouches, ornamentalists found decorative possibilities which had not existed in ancient times.

During the first half of the sixteenth century, the school of Fontainebleau provided France, and especially the enamellers of Limoges, with models of cartouches like paper scrolls, following the principle of the *carta* (see the caption accompanying the plate identified by the symbol of the *pulley*). Then, throughout Europe, the genre acquired larger proportions and began to take on the appearance of carved wood. From the second half of the sixteenth century to the first part of the seventeenth, this genre was the subject of a rivalry between artists of France, Germany and Flanders, all of whom worked to modify earlier styles in order to lend them a new grace and richness while respecting the fundamental principle of the cartouche.

Nos 5, 6 and 7.

Gilded wood reproduced from the original paintings. Nos 5 and 7 are fragments from the frames of a series of portraits of the kings of France by Dutillet, the last of which is Francis I. Magnificent manuscript, no 2848, in the Bibliothèque nationale. Both are page headings.

No 6 represents a complete miniature which we have had to reduce substantially. It is attributed to Jean Cousin. The superb manuscript from which it is borrowed was executed in the middle of the sixteenth century, for Claude Gouffier, Count of Maulevrier. It is a Book of Hours of exceptional artistic value, worthy of this enlightened patron of the arts, who died in 1570. This manuscript was part of the library of Ambroise Firmin Didot, and the page reproduced here, depicting the Adoration of the Magi, is considered the flower of the book.

Nos 2 and 9.

These fragments, inserted in the cartouches nos 1 and 8, as well as no 16, in the frame no 15, are from works by Jean Cousin and are woodcuts, similar in style to gilded woodwork.

No 15 is of comparable nature. The original is an anonymous drawing, from which we have also taken the woodwork shown as no 22.

The mirror, drawn from a photograph, belongs to the Louvre Museum. It is one of the most beautiful examples of woodcarving from the period of Francis I. The wood is not gilded, and is simply enriched with fine streaks of gold.

No 14.

A detail from the saddle of Christian II, king of Saxony. This magnificent Italian engraving, akin to goldsmith's work, is in the Museum of Dresden. Our reproduction is borrowed from the beautiful book illustrated by M. Rade published in Dresden in 1883. This cartouche has been formed in the same way as richly carved wood.

Nos 1, 8, 12 and 13.

These cartouches offer examples of the progressive transformation of the style towards the end of the sixteenth century. Nos 1 and 8 date from 1590 and are by Daniel Mayers. Nos 12 and 13 date from 1609 and most probably also belong to the Rhenish school, as does fragment no 3, which comes from the same source.

Nos 4, 10, 11, 17, 18, 19, 20 and 21.

These small cartouches and fleurons display various styles all more or less contemporary. The Rhenish taste seems to dominate among several of them.

XVIth CENTURY. XVIe SIÈCLE. XVI^tes JAHRHUNDERT

Waret, del. Imp. Firmin Didot & Cie. Paris

XVIth CENTURY.

GUIPURE LACE.

ORNAMENTATION OF HANGINGS AND CLOTHING.

Guipure lace is a combination of needlepoint and bobbin lace. It was composed of twisted silk and *cartisane*, a thin parchment covered with silk, gold, or silver thread lending relief to designs which were otherwise varied by needlework. Mary Stuart, who made guipure, gave it the name of *parchment lace*, a name well justified by borders such as our n°s 2, 3, 9, 12 and 16 which show regular patterns of edging.

Among those specimens with the largest designs, the patterns are devised so as to render the joining threads, or brides, hardly perceptible. The number of these brides increases with the degree of delicacy of the embroidery. However, artists made use of these links by arranging them in a symmetrical manner so as to integrate them with the design, as may be seen in n°s 1, 5, 6 and 13.

Of all forms of lace, guipure employed the richest materials including gold and silver threads, silks of every colour, and occasionally feathers and precious stones. In France, one finds guipure being used to decorate hangings and clothing from 1547, the year of the coronation of Henry II. Later, the inventory of Mary Stuart's wardrobe, dating from 1561–62, mentions various dresses trimmed with guipure.

From the early sixteenth century on, collections of drawings of lace patterns were printed and in the course of the century, all over Europe, masters vied with each other to provide drawings for guipure and other forms of embroidery. An infinite number of such collections were issued. Among these books, that most in vogue was by Sir Frederico da Vinciolo, dedicated to Catherine de Medici, and published in 1587. It was reprinted throughout the subsequent years, each time with new additions. Although many of these works were dedicated to both men and women, the art of guipure was mostly practised by noblewomen.

The rare volume from which we have borrowed the present examples is entitled: *Du Debvoir des filles, traicté brief, et fort utile, divisé en deux parties* ("Of the duty of girls, a brief and very useful treatise, divided into two parts"). It was published in Liège in 1597, and is by Brother Jean-Baptiste de Glen, Doctor in Theology of the University of Paris and prior of the Augustins near Liège. The first part of the book deals with the dignity of women, their good behaviour and duties, and the qualities a girl must have in order to be married, whilst the second part is concerned with the virtues of virginity and how to preserve it. The illustrations in the book were most probably borrowed from other publications.

This work was part of the library of Ambroise Firmin-Didot.

Cottelot lith Imp. Firmin-Didot & Cie Paris

XVIth–XVIIIth CENTURY.

GOLDSMITH'S WORK AND JEWELLERY.

PERSONAL ADORNMENT.

This plate is composed principally of sixteenth-century jewellery. It also contains a number of details concerning the ornamentation of European jewellery during the sixteenth and seventeenth centuries.

In these specimens, enamelled metal, engravings in niello and the use of coloured gemstones are most common. However, little has survived in terms of the actual goldwork and jewellery produced in the sixteenth century, and it is mostly from prints that such pieces are now known. Although various dandies have gathered together a wealth of these prints, they unfortunately lack those polychromatic elements which so extensively contributed to the luxury of ancient jewels.

The decorative forms intended for the adornment of the human figure can rightfully be placed alongside all other modes of ornamentation. Indeed, jewellery is one of the arts which requires the most systematic knowledge, and it has exercised the ingenuity of artists and masters of all styles throughout the ages.

XVth century.

N° 46.

Gold ring, with a stem opening out to support a setting for a diamond-shaped sapphire fastened by four claws. The stone is flanked by two dragon heads facing each other and set within flowered crowns. (Catalogue of the Louvre Museum)

XVIth century. — objects.

N° 6.

Oval medallion, rock crystal and enamelled gold. Spanish work.

N° 8.

Neck pendant. Cameo depicting the abduction of Deianeira. Enamelled gold setting, decorated with diamonds. Italian work.

N° 18.

Enamelled gold necklace, adorned with gems and pearls. Spanish work.

N° 20.

Neck pendant, enamelled gold setting, gems and pearls. Spanish work.

N°s 26 and 31.

Small pendants, enamelled gold. Of Portuguese origin.

N° 29.

Neck pendant, of enamelled gold, decorated with pearls. At the centre, a lamb made from a baroque pearl.

N° 32.

Pendant of enamelled gold, representing a horseman with a falcon on his wrist and a lady riding pillion. The costumes are from the period of Charles IX. Emerald, ruby and pearls. Like the front, the back of this jewel is enamelled with blue, red, pinkish white, green and white.

N° 35.

Pendant, the central motif of which represents the judgement of Paris, in bas relief. Enamelled gold with gems. Italian work.

N° 37.

Bouquet of moveable enamel and pearl flowers, to be worn as a brooch. This kind of jewellery is from the end of the century. Italian work.

N° 38.

Neck pendant in the shape of an eagle with a branch in his claws. Enamelled gold, with gems and pearls. Spanish work.

N° 42.

Pendant. Oval double-faced medallion, *champlevé* gold inlaid with translucent enamels and decorated with scrolls of flowers and birds. It is adorned with three natural pearls and contains the portrait of a man painted in oil on copper. French work.

N° 43.

Pendant in the shape of a ship. Gold enamelled with translucent red and green, and opaque white and blue. A silver cameo on a black ground of glass is set in each side. From the catalogue of the Louvre Museum, Italian section.

N° 49.

Pin mounting.

N° 51.

Pendant formed by a siren. In one hand she holds the arrow of love, and in the other a ruby in the shape of a crowned shield. A small winged cupid hovers above, with a floret in one hand. Enamelled gold with gems. Italian work.

N° 53.

Jewel of enamelled gold, in the shape of a lantern. The centre, of hollowed out rock crystal, contains two small religious subjects of carved wood. Spanish work.

N° 54.

Jewel of enamelled gold with a large setting which holds an octogonal topaz set in very high relief at the centre of a cartouche flanked by two seated female figures holding palms, with greyhounds. The head of a hart tops the ornament, while a grotesque mask from which a teardrop pearl is suspended adorns the bottom. A gold plaque with arabesques, insects and figurines finely engraved and enamelled in colour forms the back of the jewel. This magnificent jewel appears to have been made for Diane de Poitiers. Without the pearl, the piece is 8 centimetres high and 7 centimetres wide.

N° 59.

Neck pendant in the shape of a Latin cross turned upside down adorned with five diamonds. The setting is of enamelled gold, decorated with figures and birds. Italian work.

N°s 7 and 22.

Small pieces, one in the shape of a heart, engraved in niello, the other of an engraved escutcheon, and n°s 4 and 5, hanging pearl settings, borrowed from the work of Hans Collaert, who published two series of pendant designs, the first in 1580.

XVIIth CENTURY.

N°s 3, 14, 36, 52 and 63.

Engravings in niello from the first part of the century, in the style of J. Hurto or Hurtu, whose works, dating from 1619, are signed J.H.

N°s 13, 15, 17, 30, 39, 40, 55 and 58.

Fragments of an aigrette engraved by Gédéon Lesgaré, goldsmith in Chaumont, in his *Livre de feuilles d'orfèvrerie*, published in 1623.

N°s 21, 27, 47, 61, 62, 65 and 66.

Fragments of a similar aigrette, in a more elaborate style, also engraved. Signed: *Jean Dill, Polonois, invenit.*

N° 57.

Borrowed from the notebook of Louis Roupert, master goldsmith, in Metz.

The imitation of natural flowers which began to appear in the illumination of manuscripts in the fifteenth century did not occur in jewellery until the middle of the sixteenth century. In the course of the seventeenth century the flowers of jewellery took on a lightness and grace of appearance that imitated the whimsical liberty of nature. The aigrettes from which we have borrowed several fragments mark the peak of this incomparable, though fragile, style. The old school of Lorraine, represented in 1668 by Louis Roupert, continued to exploit the movement of natural foliage while enriching the inside with niellos, thus producing the composite features of n° 57.

N° 23.

Silver perfume flask, partly gilded. It had the capacity to hold eleven different perfumes.

N° 9, watch key: N°s 12 and 64, watchcases; N° 16, ornament support; N°s 19, 33, 48, 50 and 60, framing borders from the *Nouveau livre de boîtes et pendules, de coqs et étuis de montres et autres, par Daniel Marot, architecte*, a collection of designs for watches, clocks, watchcases, and so on.

N° 44.

Square watch, with a green and white enamel face.

XVIIIth CENTURY.

In this century, when craftsmen jewellers and goldsmiths worked to bring the whims of fashion to everybody, gold of several colours was used as well as alloys imitating gold. In 1732, Le Blanc, founder to the King, came up with a substitute for gold, *similor* and in 1758, the German Strass, successfully made fake diamonds out of a crystal which bears his name. Finally, in 1767, the fake industry had grown to such an extent that a guild of *joiaillers faussetiers* (jewellers in fakes) was established. These were necessary to satisfy the taste for luxury which had been passed from the aristocracy down to the bourgeoisie.

The first craftsman in precious metals and stones to create or follow fashion was the jewel Lempereur, whose work is recorded in engravings by Pouget, his disciple, of many small pieces, published in 1764 and 1767. It is from this collection that we have borrowed the few examples displayed here. Enamel was once again in fashion during this period.

N° 1, seal; N° 10, border of a medallion; N° 11, brooch; N° 24, pendant in the shape of a heart; N° 28, brooch; N° 34, pendant in the shape of an acorn, all from Pouget's book.

One may observe in these few models, that flowers were treated more widely than in the seventeenth century, and rendered more opulent and decorative, creating less fragile jewels.

N° 56.

Gilded silver earring, adorned with roses.

N° 45.

Seal. Baluster flanked by two consoles above an arcade holding a white agate, engraved on both sides. Catalogue of the Louvre Museum, French section.

N° 2.

Gold watch, ornamented with guilloche and enamelled in red, with a garland of engraved and enamelled ivy. The chain and key at its end are adorned with natural pearls.

N° 25.

A silver pendant, adorned with paste and coloured stones, rustic in style. It is a Norman jewel, a *holy-spirit* from the *Louis XV period* from the manufactory of Pont-Farcy, in Calvados.

N°s 35 and 51 are in the Dresden Museum. N°s 32, 43, 45 and 46 belong to the Louvre Museum. N°s 2, 8, 37, 44, 59, 54, 42, 56, 25, 6, 18, 20, 23, 25, 29, 38 and 53 are from private collections. Finally, n°s 26 and 31 are borrowed from reproductions made by Charles Revlas.

Spiégel lith.

Imp. Firmin Didot & Cie Paris

XVIIth CENTURY.

DECORATIVE TAPESTRY.

LARGE-SCALE ORNAMENTATION BASED ON GEOMETRIC PRINCIPLES.

This hanging is part of a series of tapestries which, according to tradition, was said to have been a gift from James II to Louis XIV. The series was executed in the English manufactory of Mortlake, in all likelihood after the restoration of Charles II (1660–85). However, the project appears to have been started earlier, at the time when Charles II, then still Prince of Wales, founded the factory at Mortlake, having obtained for it the famed cartoons of the *Acts of the Apostles*, painted by Raphael for Leon X, which had served as models for the Flemish weavers whose hangings are in the Vatican.

These high-warp tapestries, of silk, wool, gold, and silver are large pieces, varying in size, according to the flexibility of the subjects treated by the master. The cartoons were not always strictly followed: the model for *The Miraculous Draught of Fishes*, reproduced here, for example, was originally, in the work of Raphael, a horizontal scene. This rendition, however, is almost a perfect square, measuring 5.50 metres in height and 5.70 metres in width. The decoration of the opulent borders framing the scenes of this series is typical of the prevailing style under Louis XIII. In terms of subject-matter, proportion, and harmony between the scene and its framing border, the most felicitous of them all is by universal consent that presented here, depicting *The Miraculous Draught of Fishes*.

Each of the borders was conceived as a sort of commentary on the principal subject to which its ornamental motifs refer. In our example, a delightful swarm of cherubs with light complexions is blended with the shimmering maritime world. While the entire tapestry is reproduced here, the central scene is merely sketched out and is provided only to allow us fully to appreciate the border around it. Two fragments of the same border, reproduced on a larger scale, have also been included. The principle of light tones against dark grounds is well suited to this lively form of ornament, animated by the manifold activities of the little fishermen. Within the finely executed mouldings of the gold and marble frame, some carry large fish, others empty pots and nets, while one angel holds two keys, reminding us that one of the fishermen in the scene is Peter, who was to become the first Vicar of Christ. The flow of movement along the borders is suspended in each corner by a cartouche displaying subjects treated in gold. All four sides are divided at the centre by a motif. At the bottom, a cartouche bearing an inscription is embedded in the mouldings while the arms of England have been added at the top. This last motif is unfortunately of lesser artistic value and does not fit with the rest of the composition. Francis Crane, the first director of Mortlake, is responsible for this addition. However, nothing is known of the master-ornamentalist who composed the borders. He was most probably Flemish, of the school of Rubens, and must have studied the borders of Florentine tapestries, though the composition of the corner scenes is in keeping with the style of the school of Antwerp.

In these tapestries, the balance between border and central subject was not achieved at random. On the contrary, their proportions were devised according to a precise geometric formula, illustrated below. A circle containing a perfect

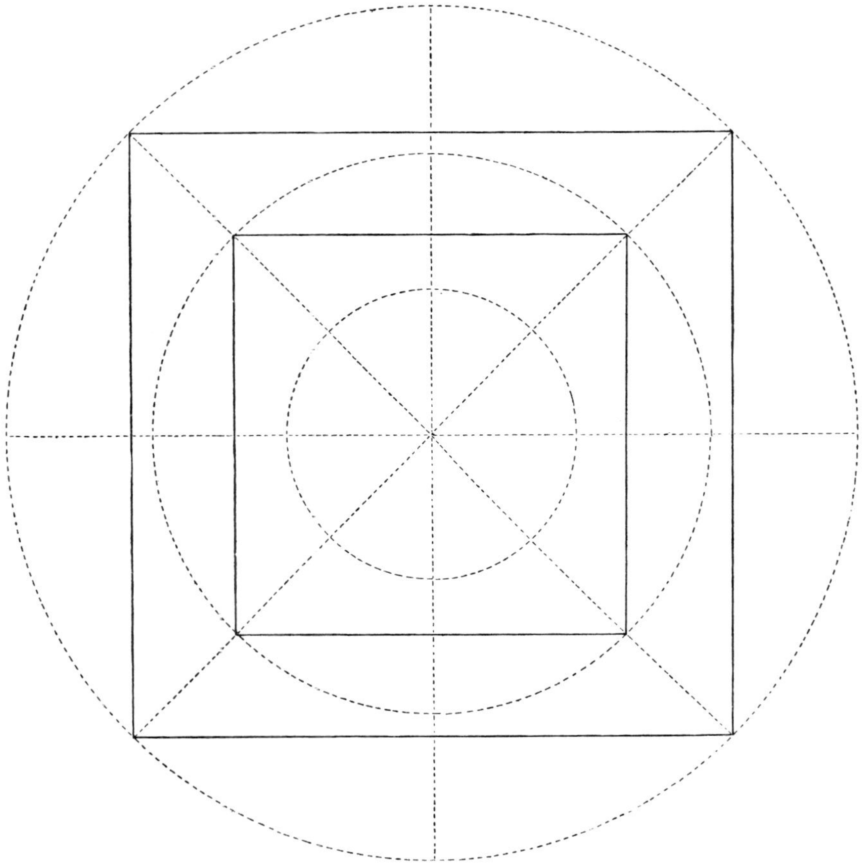

square is subdivided into three equal parts, from the centre to the circumference. The point at which the diagonal axis of the square meets the second inner circle determines the width of the border. In the tapestry at hand, though the square is not perfect, the same principle has been followed, as shown in the second geometric figure below. Here the original figure is divided into two parts which are then reassembled according to the new proportions.

Furthermore, through the careful choice of the ornamental motifs for the uprights of the border, mostly vertical figures, the artist has attempted to impart to this work the illusory appearance of a perfect square.

PONTVM SVDAT
LABOR OMNIS INANIS
ARTE LABOR
EN CHRISTVS IN ALTV
IPSE CAPIT

XVIIth CENTURY.

MURAL PAINTINGS. — ORNAMENTATION OF WAINSCOTTS.

TAPESTRIES AND PANELLING. — CORNERS AND BORDERS.

In the original, these three panels, painted on wood, are 2.40 metres in height. In the absence of more precise information, they are attributed to Simon Vouet, as they indeed display several features typical of the decorative concepts of this master-painter in whose workshop many artists were schooled, including Le Sueur, Le Brun and Mignard, who often collaborated with him. He himself had learned his trade in good hands.

Born in Paris in 1590, Simon Vouet died there in 1649. He had spent fifteen years in Italy, first in Venice where he learned the style of Veronese, then in Rome where he was put in charge of the decoration of several churches, and finally in Genoa. At the request of Louis XIII he returned to France in 1627, with the experience both of the vigorous style of Caravaggio, and of the calmer and lighter style of Guido Reni. Named first painter to the King and housed in the Louvre, Simon Vouet became the superintendent, as it were, of the fine arts of the period, a role he was well equipped to fulfil, and which he would eventually pass on to Le Brun.

Simon Vouet, whose output was immense, designed many tapestries, and executed large works in the royal residencies, including the castle of Fontainebleau, where one ornamental panel painted by his hand remains in good condition. The points in common between this panel and our examples allow us to attribute the latter at the very least to artists of his school, or to a member of his family, which produced generations of artists.

These three panels are evidence of modifications to the Renaissance style, to which they nevertheless owe their fundamental character. In this new genre, heaviness is combined with delicacy in ornamental constructions, which the painter enriches with all kinds of elements. These include the marble of architectural sculptures, painted or gilded wood, carved in all possible styles, the human figure, along with chimeras and grotesques, quadrupeds, birds, butterflies, the classical acanthus scroll, natural flowers, masks, vases, or fine ribbons attached in singular fashion to an ethereal ground. The motif in the central medallion represents Jupiter being suckled by the goat Amalthea, and indeed mythological subjects were very much in vogue at the time. Large compositions of this kind were ruled by the order of symmetry, which, coupled with the delicate silhouettes of the foliage inherited from the Renaissance, soon to be lost to the growing taste for opulence, lends clarity to this ornamental style.

The two corner motifs which are fragments of tapestry borders were also displayed in an exhibition held in Paris in 1876. They are in the style of the late seventeenth and early eighteenth centuries. The corner with a damasked ground for which we have not provided colour, is from a series of tapestries by Coypel on the adventures of Don Quixote. In the series, the grounds vary: the damask pattern is yellow or crimson.

Picard, lith.

Imp. Firmin-Didot & Cie Paris

XVIth–XVIIth CENTURY.

LARGE-SCALE ORNAMENTATION.

CORNERS AND BORDERS OF TAPESTRIES.

Of these border ornaments, one is from the manufactory of Mortlake, in England, while the others are from Parisian workshops.

According to the catalogue of the exhibition of tapestries organized by the Union centrale des arts décoratifs at the Palace of the Champs-Elysées in 1876, there existed in Paris, from 1570 to 1660, a manufactory of tapestries, designated the *Fabrique royale de Paris* (Royal Factory of Paris) of which the Flemish artist Charles Coomans was the director when he died in 1634, leaving the factory in the hands of his brother Alexandre. This was a separate establishment from the manufactory of high-warp tapestries, the *Fabrique royale*, founded by Henry IV in 1610, housed first in the place Royale before it was moved to the neighbourhood of the Gobelins, in around 1630. The establishment, which is known historically under the name of *manufacture des Gobelins*, dates from 1662, and was organized during the ministry of Colbert. In addition to tapestries, all the decorative furniture intended for the royal palaces was made there. The influential painter C. Le Brun was the first director of the establishment.

N° 6.

Fabrique Royale de Paris.

Border of the first piece of the Artemisia series of six hangings. Wool and silk tapestry, 3.85 metres in height, 5.20 metres in width.

N° 2.

Mortlake manufactory.

Border of the second piece of the Vulcan series of five hangings. Silk, wool, gold and silver tapestry, 4.30 metres high and 5.80 metres wide. The border bears the initials FC, for Francis Crane, the first director of the Mortlake factory, which was founded by Charles I before 1625, when he was still Prince of Wales.

N° 3.

Fabrique royale.

Corner and part of the border of a silk and wool tapestry representing the *Hunt of Meleager*. This border is signed with two enlaced Cs, which may be the mark of Charles Coomans.

N° 4.

Manufacture des Gobelins.

Side border in the style of Jean Lepautre.

We have listed the motifs above in the most probable chronological order, according to the style of the cartouches.

N°s 1 and 5 are supplementary fragments taken from the border frames of the collection of medals struck in honour of Louis XIV. This small-scale ornamentation, of a mixed style, is from the end of the seventeenth century.

Brandin, lith.
Imp. Firmin Didot & Cie Paris

XVIIth CENTURY.

LARGE DECORATIVE COMPOSITIONS.

ORNAMENTATION OF THE SPRINGING OF AN ARCH, SCULPTED AND PAINTED.

The fragment reproduced here is from the arched ceiling of the Apollo Gallery in the Louvre.

After the fire of 1661 which had destroyed the first gallery started under Charles IX and finished under Henry IV, Louis XIV entrusted Le Brun with the new decoration which has remained to this day. Le Brun was then still under the influence of the Italian style learned from his master, Nicolas Poussin.

Le Brun devised the entire ornamental scheme of the gallery, including the choice of compositions to be painted, the invention of sculptured figures, the synchronization of the ornaments and the significance of the symbols. It is well known that Louis XIV had selected Apollo, the god of light and of the arts, as his symbol and that his emblem was a sun shining over a world, with these words: *nec pluribus impar* ("Unequal to the multitude"). It is this allegorical image which inspired Le Brun who merged in one god Homer's *Helios*, the Sun of the Romans, son of Hyperion and Thea, and the *Apollo* of the Greeks, son of Zeus and Leto.

Various allusions to both divinities are ingeniously distributed throughout the ornamental composition. In the upper corners of our fragment, for example, the face of the sun appears with the motto of Louis XIV while the opposite corner displays the lyre of Apollo with two cornucopias. The celestial character of the ceiling is evident in the names of the constellations inscribed on the blue grounds of cartouches distributed throughout the whole. *Leo* and *Virgo*, visible in our fragment, recall the forty-five and forty-eight stars which make up those signs.

Le Brun divided the barrel vault into eleven cartouches or principal compartments. In the central one, he proposed to represent Apollo on his chariot, with all the attributes of the sun. The *Seasons* were to occupy the four neighbouring cartouches. Two ovals were to depict *evening* and *morning* while two octagonal compartments further removed would have represented *night* and *dawn*. The *Waking of the Waters* and the *Waking of the Earth* under the first rays of the sun were to adorn either end of the vault.

However, Le Brun was named director of the manufactory of the Gobelins in 1662, and then became absorbed in the large project to which Louis XIV assigned him at Versailles so that he never finished the Apollo Gallery at the Louvre, which was completed only recently. The style exhibited here, which we will call his early style, is more typical of the period and of superior artistic interest than the loud and lavish ornamentation which triumphed twenty years later in the Grande Galerie at Versailles.

Nordmann lith. Imp. Firmin Didot & Cie Paris

XVIIth CENTURY.

LARGE-SCALE ORNAMENTATION.

CARPET AND TAPESTRY BORDER.

These motifs are from the most brilliant period of the decorative arts under Louis XIV. The large one is from a carpet which is 8.90 metres long and 3.90 metres wide. It is part of a series of thirteen pieces intended for the floor of the Apollo Gallery in the Louvre. The intensity of the colours is especially suited to the use of wool.

In the notice accompanying the plate identified by the symbol of the *harpoon*, depicting a fragment of the ornamentation of the arch of the Apollo Gallery, we mentioned the care with which Le Brun planned the entire decorative scheme of the gallery. Carpets were included in this large-scale plan.

The border fragment is from the cycle of fourteen tapestries relating the *History of Louis XIV* made in the manufactory of the Gobelins. Each scene, designed by Le Brun, is framed by a similar border. Our corner fragment conveys the general colour scheme of this ornamental border. The tapestries are made of wool, silk, silver and gold.

Méheux lith.

Imp. Firmin Didot & Cie Paris

XVIIth CENTURY.

LUXURY FURNITURE. — METAL MARQUETRY.

Metal marquetry dates only from the second half of the seventeenth century. Metal, widely used in the furniture of Antiquity, is absent from Medieval furniture, whilst it remains a rarity in sixteenth century works.

Under Louis XIV, the wood of furniture was inlaid with tortoiseshell and bright metals in order to keep in step with the luxury of the palaces. And it was at the hands of Charles-André Boulle that this style of furniture was to attain the height of perfection.

The piece displayed here, a *secrétaire*, is at present in the Apollo Gallery in the Louvre. It is of the noble character typical of the productions of the manufactory of the Gobelins under the direction of Le Brun. The straight lines of the architectural design as well as the style of decoration are evidence of the revival of Roman Antiquity, so thoroughly studied by Nicolas Poussin. This style belongs to the initial period of the manufactory of the Gobelins and is still devoid of the fancy appendages that were to typify its productions under the direction of Mignard, after the death of Le Brun in 1696.

André-Charles Boulle, *ébéniste du Roi* (cabinetmaker to the King), was also a qualified architect, sculptor and engraver. This is quite apparent in the example shown in our plate. The design of this piece is the work of an architect, whilst the gilded bronzes are those of a fine sculptor. The techniques of engraving were used for the ribs of the metal foliage.

Furniture in this style enjoyed great favour at the end of the seventeenth and beginning of the eighteenth centuries. Strangely enough for France, the taste for this genre did not decline: the *Encyclopédie* states that "it was abandoned only because of the time required to produce works of this kind."

The remaining objects and fragments in the plate are of a similar type.

N°s 2, 3, 4 and 5, are borrowed from the engravings of goldwork by Ludovicus Cossinus. Here, the metal is engraved and glazed in the manner of niellowork.

N°s 7 and 9, cases by Daniel Marot.

N° 6, snuffbox inlaid with gold and silver, taken from a book by Du Vivier, 1719–20.

N° 8, top of a box, designer unknown.

Spiegel lith.

Imp. Firmin-Didot & Cie Paris

XVIIth CENTURY.

CABINETWORK DECORATED WITH GILDED ENGRAVINGS AND METAL MARQUETRY.

In order to illustrate the variety of furniture produced by Charles-André Boulle at the manufactory of the Gobelins when it was under the direction of Le Brun, a second piece is shown on this plate. This one is an *armoire* and is an architectonic piece *par excellence*. It alone would justify the title of architect mentioned in Boulle's certificate of apprenticeship.

The rectangular motif with a lock, in the lower part of the plate, is the decoration of a *secrétaire* drawer. It is repeated on the ten drawers of the piece, which are horizontally arranged, with a panel in the middle, the frame of which is supported by claws while the upper part is decorated with a horizontal trophy. Five drawers are superimposed vertically on each side. It is a variant of the piece displayed in the plate identified by the symbol of the *pencil holder*. This *secrétaire* is part of the collection of the Mobilier National. The two rosettes are decorations on the tops of powder boxes. They are borrowed from the "*Nouveaux dessins pour graver sur l'orfèvrerie, inventés et gravés par le sieur Masson*" ("New designs for engraving on gold, invented and engraved by Mr Masson"). This inferior style of ornamentation, derived from the manner of Bérain, dates from the first part of the eighteenth century.

Spiégel, lith. Imp. Firmin Didot & Cie, Paris

XVIIth CENTURY

METAL MARQUETRY.

This console, drawn from a photograph and now displayed in the Apollo Gallery at the Louvre, is also the work of Charles-André Boulle. It is more discreetly decorated with carving and the marquetry is its principal ornamentation.

The plan of the console included below is useful in demonstrating the role of the bottom shelf in unifying the piece and in pointing out the position of the legs, the axis of which is slightly different from front to back in order to modify the perspective and give the console an appearance of greater depth.

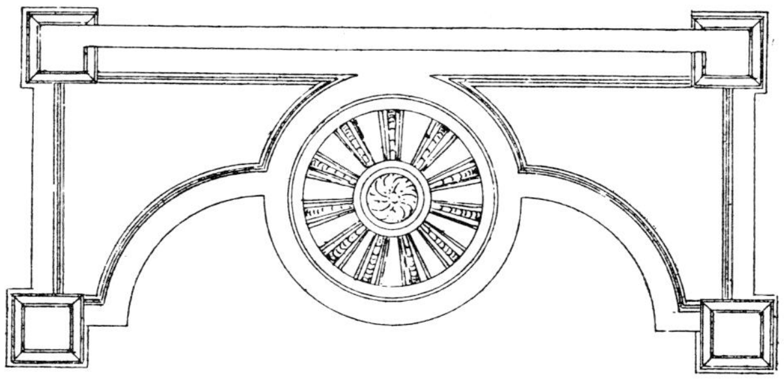

The ornamental technique of this piece is referred to as *contre-partie* (or contre-Boulle) marquetry as opposed to *première partie* (or Boulle marquetry). The latter consists of a ground of tortoiseshell inlaid with a pattern of brass. In the former a pattern cut in the sheet of brass which forms the ground is inlaid with tortoiseshell. While Boulle marquetry was more highly prized, our example illustrates the subtle possibilities of contre-Boulle marquetry.

Among the organic materials used in marquetry were tortoiseshell, horn, ivory and mother-of-pearl. The metals most commonly used include brass, pewter, silver and gold. Not only the metal parts but also the flattened tortoiseshell could be engraved, and once the engravings were made, black mastic and melted rosin were applied to the cuttings to make them visible.

The white element in our example is pewter, an alloy with which Boulle worked wonders. Its surface has been treated with chemicals so as to lend it pearly iridescent tones which complement the sheen of the polished ebony.

The engravings of patterns cut from sheets of brass displayed at the bottom of our plate, signed by Daudet, one of the masters of the period, were intended as models for craftsmen.

Spiegel lith. Imp. Firmin Didot & Cie Paris

XVIIth CENTURY

DECORATIVE PAINTINGS AND MINIATURES.

The horizontal and the upright friezes, n[os] 1 and 5, are suitable for architectural ornamentation. The initials and the cartouche are illuminations from large-format choir books.

The Deer Hunt and *The Triumph of Neptune* are taken from the *Œuvres d'architecture de Jean Lepautre* (The architectural works of Jean Lepautre). the first motif is part of a series entitled *Frises, feuillages et ornaments à l'italienne* (Friezes, foliage and ornaments in the Italian style). It dates from around 1660. The second is from another series, *Montants à l'antique* (Uprights in the antique style), dated 1659.

In *The Deer Hunt*, the tumultuous activity of the hunters, angels, dogs and deer, painted in full colour, is tempered by the colossal ornamental foliage treated *en camaieu*, the size of which helps to unify the composition.

The animation of the upright frieze differs from that of the horizontal motif. Its triumphal character does not allow for the same passion, yet it calls for more vibrant colours.

Jean Lepautre was one of the most devoted collaborators of Le Brun at the manufactory of the Gobelins, from the time of its establishment in 1662. Our examples show how accomplished an artist Lepautre already was, a man whose ardour Le Brun must have had to temper. Indeed, it is only in engravings such as these, coloured by the artist himself or following his recommendations that the true spirit of Lepautre emerges. In the works produced in collaboration with Le Brun, it is exceedingly difficult to distinguish his contribution.

N[os] 3 and 7 are taken from the borders of tapestries of the same period.

Next to the mastery of Lepautre, miniatures such as n[os] 2, 4, 6, 8 and 9 can only be of modest appearance. Nevertheless, it is quite apparent that the great opulence of architectural ornamentation engendered similar opulence in the decoration of manuscripts. These miniatures, though they still belong to the seventeenth century by their style, date from the very end of the seventeenth and the early years of the eighteenth centuries. By this time, because of the development of engraving, miniatures painted in books had steadily become more and more rare. The originals of those displayed here are found in an Antiphonary in four volumes. This book of antiphons, which is 0.83 metres in height and 0.59 metres in width, was produced in the monastery of Sainte-Geneviève in Paris for the church of Saint-Vincent in Senlis. Started in 1705, it was not completed until 1729. Our examples are signed by a canon, Antoine Gervaix, who worked on this manuscript in 1706, continuing a work first composed of ornamental paintings of the seventeenth century. His style is perfectly in keeping with earlier illumination.

Brandin, lith.

Imp. Firmin-Didot & Cie Paris

XVIIth–XVIIIth CENTURY.

DECORATIVE TAPESTRY AND MINIATURES.

This tapestry, 3.75 metres in height and 2.50 metres in width, is typical of a style common at the end of the seventeenth and early eighteenth centuries which favoured as subjects the legendary gods and allegories of the elements, the seasons and the months of the year. These cycles of hangings were part of the winter furnishings of apartments and were replaced by taffeta in the summer. The example shown here was recently displayed in an exhibition in Paris. It belongs to a transitional style between the ornamentation of the second half of the seventeenth century and that of the Regency period.

In these compositions, more or less architectonic in appearance, fantasy, though still subjected to the symmetry of a general scheme, was beginning to affirm itself. The taste and fancy of the ornamentalist gradually took precedence over architectural conventions and the elements of the construction took on the aspect of delicate wainscots to which wall hangings had been fixed, a style of which Jean Bérain had made frequent use. The delicacy of the ornamental composition apparent in the example in our plate indicates that it is from the school of Gillot. His hand is recognizable in the composition of the piece, in the treatment of the figures, and in the use of straightforward background colours. Bérain, the teacher of Watteau, was an ingenious innovator. The articulation of this motif is the early manifestation of a fashion that was to lead to garlanded mirror frames with uprights fashioned like bending palms. The delicacy with which the illusory carved wood is treated prefigures the fine carving of mouldings of the Louis XV style.

These sumptuous tapestries were made with wool, silk, gold and sometimes silver. Among the craftsmen who executed these hangings the name of Audran figures prominently. Surrounding the central motif is a squared damask design of metallic threads.

The large fragment, taken from the border of an illuminated page, obeys the principle of a painted carved wood frame. An example of this nature, true to the style of its time, provides valuable information regarding the use of colour during that period.

The initials in our plate go with the initials and cartouche displayed in the plate identified by the symbol of the *trousers*. They are taken from the same source: the *Antiphonaire à l'usage de Saint-Vincent de Senlis* in four volumes, which was illuminated between 1705 and 1729 in the monastery of Sainte-Geneviève in Paris. One of these initials is set against a blue monochrome landscape, a commonly used style at the time. The overall style of these motifs is representative of the seventeenth century.

Brandin, lith.

Imp. Firmin-Didot & Cie Paris

XVIIth AND XVIIIth CENTURIES.

BORDERS OF TAPESTRIES, FRAGMENTS.

The first motif, starting from the top of the plate, is a cartouche from the lower border of a hanging which is one of a cycle recounting the story of Jason and Medea, after De Troy. The border imitates a gilded rocaille frame. This high-warp tapestry of wool and silk is signed G. Audran, 1751. Manufactory of the Gobelins.

The second fragment is from the series of tapestries known as the Constantine hangings, part of which is attributed to Jules Romain, while the rest is believed to be the work of Rubens. These tapestries of wool, silk, gold and silver, were manufactured by the Fabrique royale de Paris, circa 1610.

The third motif is a fragment from the border of a series of eighteen tapestries. The models for this cycle, which recounts the story of the life of Esther, were created by De Troy. The tapestries themselves were executed by Cozette and by Monmerque, between 1738 and 1752. High warp, wool, silk. Manufactory of the Gobelins.

The fourth fragment belongs to a sequence of nine pieces, known as the story of Alexander, after Le Brun. The borders of this series are varied. The large foliated volutes around a strip of flowers shown here recur in several of them. High-warp tapestry, wool, silk, silver and gold. Manufactory of the Gobelins.

The fifth strip is a clothing ornament borrowed from the second piece of the Artemisia cycle, after Antoine Caron. This tapestry, of wool and silk, was made in the Fabrique royale de Paris, towards the end of the sixteenth century.

The originals of these documents were exhibited in Paris in 1876 by the Union centrale des arts décoratifs.

XVIIe SIÈCLE

XVIIth CENTURY XVII^tes JAHRHUNDERT.

Brandin, lith. Imp. Firmin-Didot & Cie, Paris

XVIIIth CENTURY.

DECORATIVE PANEL.

CORNERS AND BORDERS OF TAPESTRIES.

The central illustration on our plate, entitled the *Triumph of Pomona*, the goddess of fruits, is a composition by François Boucher, engraved by Cochin, which belongs to the pastoral genre. It is an engraving of some size, measuring over fifty centimetres in height, and dates from approximately 1735, when the career of Boucher was in full flourish. Indeed, as early as 1724, whilst barely 20 years of age, he had been awarded the first prize of the Academy of Painting. However, this sketch may date from an earlier time, closer to his youth; for one is bound to acknowledge, upon the examination of this composition, that in the ornamentation properly so called, Boucher employed only elements of existing styles, the particular nature of which he borrowed from various artists. In this respect, it is possible that Boucher may always have proceeded thus. Here, the artist employs the borrowed elements without blending them, each separate genre serving a specific purpose, and their bold combination creating a rich decorative whole.

Considered from this point of view, this panel offers one of those models, fashioned by an artist of genius, from which new styles emerge. When this composition was sketched by Boucher, the decorative style subsequently known as the Louis XV style, truly came into being and the painter provided from the outset a freedom and a sense of fantasy unknown before him, which are one of its most attractive expressions.

The upper part of the panel shows an open space, with behind it a house hidden by trees, whilst a landscape forms the background of the scene. This part of the composition differs greatly from the opulent ornamentation which serves as a base to the whole. The central scene serves as a link between both parts.

Boucher borrowed the character of the upper part of the panel, comprising the landscape and the suspended crown, from the delicate school of Gillot, which Watteau also followed in his ornamentations.

The cartouche decorating a sort of pedestal, which serves as a projecting base to the ornamental construction, is pure Meissonnier. Boucher has also borrowed from this artist the opening he made in it, in the background of which a pool and a fine fountain are represented, their water trickling into the foreground, through the curves of the aperture, hereby creating a most felicitous effect of movement. The only direct references to Antiquity in the entire composition are the type of architecture standing in the background of the pool, and the head of the faun guarding the fountain, treated by the painter with a breadth akin to that of the grotesques of the Pont-Neuf.

It is on this base that Boucher has displayed his pastoral subject, which his contemporaries referred to as his *fouillis* ("jumble") — not in a pejorative sense, but rather to suggest its decorative opulence. The scene depicts two figures, a young man and a young woman, sorting out vegetables and fruits, whilst a third person, another young woman, watches the scene resting her elbow upon the back of a mule. The composition is set in a bright and high-contrast light, unlike the softer tones of the trees and landscape in the background, and it projects out of the narrow opening. This is clearly indicated by the leaning tree which appears in the foreground.

In this work the artist has broken old moulds, bring new and, before him, unknown possibilities to ornamentation. He has given fresh life to traditional themes: the title of the panel, *The Triumph of Pomona*, recalls only distantly the preceding century when statues of Pomona and Vertumna were placed in the groves of Versailles. Indeed, after Watteau, who had rejected the pompous boredom and the majesty of the *Grand Siècle* and of the Sun King, preferring the atmosphere of gallant comedians in untamed nature, Boucher was not concerned in the least with the actual representation of the two Roman gods in his scene.

A Parisian, he had acquired a taste for the country and for peasants, with the pleasant disorder of their dwellings, farm-yards and pens, in the outskirts of his native town. This sincere predilection, Boucher communicates with the conviction of an artist who is confident in the charm of the things he depicts.

There is in this sketch (which may or may not have been the basis for a painting) a youthful vigour, a verve and boldness which give it a particular value. The artist became more moderate with time, as one may judge by the ornamental decoration of the tapestry represented in the plate identified by the symbol of the *balloon*.

With the ornamental style of the epoch of Louis XV, France recovered an independance in its national genius, which had suffered since Gothic times; and Boucher is amongst those who expressed French taste in its true originality with the most success.

Corners and borders of tapestries.

The borders of eighteenth-century tapestries appear most like frames in gilded woodwork of a similar nature to those of paintings. The gilding was applied in various tones and blended, from time to time, with discreet applications of paint. As a rule, the corner motif is always set inside the frame.

In addition to this type of border in which the sides are of uniform width, forming a regular frame, there are also borders with sculpted inner sides. The interest of this technique resides in the blending of the border decoration with that of the tapestry. Ch. Coypel employed it to great effect in the series of tapestries entitled "Don Quixote". This type is exemplified on our plate by fragment n° 2, which is both rich and delicate.

All these examples which were produced by the manufactories of the Gobelins and of Beauvais, were displayed at the Palace of the Champs-Elysées in 1876, by the Union centrale des arts décoratifs.

1 2 3 4 5

Sᵗ Elme Gautier del. Nordmann, lith.

Imp. Firmin-Didot & Cⁱᵉ, Paris

XVIIIth CENTURY.

TAPESTRIES, HANGINGS, AND CORNERS OF BORDERS.

The principal motif on our plate represents one of the four hangings which make up the series known as the *Sujets de la Fable*, manufactured by the Gobelins from Boucher's designs, with the ornamental areas designed by Tessier. The composition dates from 1757. These tapestries measure 4.25 metres in height.

The present hanging looks like a portion of a wall decorated in Rococo style. It comprises a central medallion depicting Aurora and Cephalus, encompassed by an oval frame in gilded wood, which is suspended from an inner frame on a ground of pink silk. This inner frame is adorned with a border of silk of the same type as the preceding one, but of a much darker tone. The entire composition is encompassed within a rich rectangular frame, also in gilded wood.

A vase, similar to those produced in Sèvres, is placed in the middle of the outer frame, which serves as a stand. Manifold garlands of flowers, as well as perched or fluttering birds, a porcupine, and even a monkey armed with a sporting-gun, animate this scene with their colours and their movement. The composition would have been entirely conceived in *trompe-l'oeil*, if the garlands and the creatures had cast their shadows on the background as does the oval frame in the centre.

The two corners of borders are from the manufactory of Beauvais. The border designed to resemble a gilded frame adorned with oak-leaves, serves as a frame to a grotesque hanging, in the style of Bérain. This ornamentation must therefore date from the first part of the eighteenth century. The other frame, with its corner-stone cartouche adorned with a fleur-de-lis, dates from the time of Louis XV.

Gaulard. lith. Imp Firmin Didot & Cie. Paris

XVIIIth CENTURY.

ORNAMENTATION OF WOODEN WAINSCOTS: GILDED SCULPTURES, MOULDINGS AND TROPHIES.

The originals shown in this plate are from the Château of Versailles, where they are found in the *petits appartements* of Louis XV. It is known that this king, weary of living in the vast suite of rooms used by Louis XIV, had a large section of the old palace transformed into a comfortable dwelling, in which he could throw off the yoke of the old etiquette. The change was profound in all respects, and a new style of architecture and of decoration replaced the style of Mansart, Lepautre, Marot, and Bérain. Robert de Cotte had shown the first signs of this change, and after him came Boffrand, Coutant and Cartaud, who created a new form of architecture, from which an entirely original decorative art emerged, free of any preoccupation with Antiquity, and devoid of foreign influence. The movement was widespread. One senses the impetuosity of a national character in the process of recovering its liberty and freeing itself from the Italian Renaissance.

Various epochs of the Louis XV style may be distinguished; n°s 1, 2, 3, 4, 6 and 7, which are ornamentations of perfect taste and of excellent workmanship, belong to its best period.

Wood painted white, with gilded ornaments was the material most often employed, since it offered the greatest brilliancy, as may be seen in our examples n°s 1, 2, 3, 4 and 6. These decorative features are taken from the drawing-room of Madame Adélaïde, daughter of Louis XV, which is one of the most richly decorated rooms of the *petits appartements*, as all the ornamentation is made of gilded and carved wood and stucco. The work dates from approximately 1750, that is, the highpoint of the formation of the Louis XV style, and is presumed to be by Verberckt. The graceful carvings on the wainscots in the *petits appartements*, as well as the carved gilded brass works, were in fact fashioned by a whole group of artists, most of whom are unknown to us.

The trophies on our plate are composed of a variety of elements: n°s 1 and 3 are made up of musical instruments, whilst fishing equipment makes up n° 2, and gardening tools n° 4. Each one of these is adorned with a winged cartouche, depicting children using the implements displayed.

N°s 5 and 8, both of which adorn a wainscot set between two book-cases, are in a somewhat modified style, as each group of ornaments is distinctly separate. This style recalls the hanging flowers and fruits in a series of bouquets found in Raphael's decorations in the Vatican. They are evidence of the emergence of the Louis XVI style. N° 5 is dedicated to music, pastorale and dance, whilst n° 8 is dedicated to comedy, satire, burlesque and epic poetry.

Durin, lith.

Imp. Firmin Didot & Cie, Paris

XVIIIth CENTURY.

DECORATIVE TAPESTRIES.

BAS-RELIEFS AND MEANDERS.

Of these two tapestries, the larger one is displayed in its entirety, the other has been reduced. Their clear, free and fully ornamental features differ substantially from those of tapestries of earlier times, including those of the first part of the eighteenth century itself. During that century the art of tapestry underwent a revolution resulting from the widespread use of delicately and richly sculptured wooden mouldings in interior domestic decoration. The superfluity of ornament created by placing inside a real frame adorned with reliefs a tapestry which had its own woven border designed to resemble another frame adorned with reliefs, produced such an unhappy effect that in some tapestries the woven border was completely removed, as in the examples in our plate. Otherwise, a woven border in a flat tone separated the white ground from the gilding of the frame. Lastly, the decoration became completely ornamental, abounding in scrolls of foliage, garlands of flowers, medallions, fluttering Cupids, birds, and so on.

The upper tapestry on our plate belongs to what was called the "*noble pastorale*" because of the allegories depicted in it. It is decorated with a pair of medallions, set facing one another: the first one, with its barren landscape and the warm fire of its brazier, is an allegory of winter, whilst the other is an allegory of fruitful summer. Between the two medallions a set of agricultural tools are represented, including a rake, a pitchfork, a watering can, a wheat-basket and a sieve.

The other pastoral scene is entitled: "The Offering to Love". It depicts the statue of Cupid aiming his bow at the heart of a beautiful woman, who expresses only gratitude to her victor, whilst a young man renders to the god the homage of his victory.

These pretty, slightly contrived creations, in which use was made of both silk and wool, the latter for shades and half-tones and silk for highlights, are amongst the best produced by the manufactory of Beauvais.

The motifs in bas-relief date from the time of Louis XVI. Although they are related to the patterns of Antiquity, artists such as Lafosse, Londe and Huet retained an independence in their compositions, conferring upon them a truly French character, as may be seen from the two large fragments in the middle of our plate. The other motifs display the standard types of running patterns.

The tapestries were part of the 1876 exhibition organized in the Palace of the Champs-Elysées by the Union centrale des arts décoratifs.

Brandin, lith.

Imp. Firmin Didot & Cie Paris

XVIIIth CENTURY.

PAINTING UNDER GLASS, AGE OF LOUIS XVI.

These panels are from the jewellery cabinet presented in 1787 to Queen Marie-Antoinette by the city of Paris. This mahogany cabinet is considered to be one of the French masterpieces of the genre.

The panels are simply painted on paper, with glass applied to create the illusion that the paintings were directly enamelled. Degault, who made these panels, used this technique with great skill. He endowed his decoration with a discreet richness, the quality of which could scarcely be equalled by direct painting on glass.

The style of these panels is derived from the main source of inspiration at that time, the Pompeiian style. The rule of symmetry is respected, and treated with true grace. The figures representing half maidens, half acanthus leaves, are particularly worthy of note. Under-glass painting is itself an ancient technique.

The jewellery cabinet of Marie-Antoinette has been placed in the bathroom of Napoleon I, at Saint-Cloud and then at Compiègne. In 1830, it was at the Palace of the Tuileries; today it is in the Petit-Trianon, at Versailles.

Mauler, lith. Imp. Firmin-Didot & Cie. Paris.

XIXth CENTURY.

CONTINUOUS GROUNDS COMPOSED OF FLOWERS AND FOLIAGE:

FABRICS AND WALLPAPER.

Harmony results from variety in unity. In order to achieve unity in a variety of assembled colours, it is necessary to have an assimilating tone which predominates. That is to say that this tone, which serves as a link between the colours, absorbs the individual vividness of each one of them for the benefit of the whole.

In the samples gathered here we find examples of the variations in chromatic scales; examples which judiciously abide by the rules of common proportion in form and colour. These specimens are the very models of designs printed on fabric. One senses in them the skill and experience of a true master. Though reduced in size, their true formation is accurately reproduced.

These examples date from the first half of the nineteenth century.

P. Lestel, lith. Imp. Firmin Didot & Cie Paris

XIXth CENTURY.

ORNAMENTATION OF PRINTED FABRIC.

CONTINUOUS GROUNDS OF THE PLANT PRINCIPLE.

These documents form a continuation to those which make up the plate identified by the symbol of the *pitcher*. They are also models for the decoration of wool muslin, reproduced from original designs. It is appropriate to examine these specimens in the specific light of the manufacturing technique for which these models are designed. Wool muslin is not one of those fabrics which is made to look shiny by laying on it a substance which sets off its colour. Its relative dullness partly absorbs the intensity of the tones, and thus the most vivid opposites always retain a certain harmony. In his design, the artist can therefore enhance the intensity of the tones to be printed, knowing full well that they will be dulled by the fabric.

The flora of our gardens and fields has never been better known than today, and it is with delightful simplicity that these decorations have been composed of pansies, daisies, convolvuluses, sweet peas, narcissi, and of course roses. However, the decorative skills with which these flowers have been represented are not those which generate new ornamental styles. Indeed, the nineteenth century, in its enlightened eclectism, rejecting nothing of the past but trying in turn, as it were, all the different formulas of the ages, has not yet truly invented a style of its own, which may be historically classified as such.

Lestel, lith.

Imp. Firmin Didot & Cie Paris

To end this collection of historical documents, we have added here a reproduction of one of the most sumptuous decorative arrangements dating from the latter part of our century. This neo-Greek ornamentation, the elements of which are sculptured, both actually and in *trompe-l'oeil*, adorns the ceiling of the hall of the *Sept Cheminées*, in the Palace of the Louvre. Its discreet colouring was specifically required to avoid the possibility of any unwarranted brightness detracting from the paintings displayed in this room, which is lit from the ceiling. Duban, who designed the whole decor, was the architect of the Louvre in 1850.